Don + Phyllis -
Thanks for twenty years of
basketball. We'd be overweight
couch potatoes if it weren't for
Here's to a more just + peace
Brian 9.3.06

Sequestered

Brian Solomon

Goblin Fern Press

Madison, Wisconsin

Published by Goblin Fern Press, Inc.
6401 Odana Road, Suite B
Madison, WI 53719
www.goblinfernpress.com
Toll-free: 888-670-BOOK (2665)
Quantity discounts available from the publisher.

10-digit ISBN: 0-9722099-3-X
13-digit ISBN: 978-0-9722099-3-9
LCCN: 2004113234

Cover illustration by Tom Lowes.
Cover design by Ken Crocker and GFP Design.

A portion of the proceeds from the sale of this book will go to support Jennifer and Jacob Kutz, who have lost their mother but not her memory.

A portion will also go to Domestic Abuse Intervention Services (DAIS), to help us reach a time when no family ever has to endure this again.

Printed in the United States.
First printing.

For Kaiya:

Thanks for reminding me

what is important.

The search for truth is not an easy one. What is truth, really, but an image of fact, a picture of reality, in one's mind? Truth is ever-changing and always relative. One man's truth is another's tall tale. The search for truth is an individual one, and each individual must develop his own strategy.

The search for truth is not a journey down a well-lit path; it is more a blind reach combined with the hope that your hand will clutch something worthwhile.

In my search for truth, I often closed my eyes and imagined another place where I could clutch something worthwhile. Beth, I know you as if you were my own sister. I see you here, in this place, where you in-line skate and laugh, fly your kite, wash your car, ride on the back of Dave's motorcycle, take pictures, drink a beer, and enjoy your children, Jacob and Jennifer.

I might seem strange to you because we've never actually met, but I know you well. I am quite fond of you and am truly happy, after what seems like years, to finally meet you. In this story, in this place, the ending is always a good one.

I can find truth here.

Ellen, Greg, Dave, Tom, and Vern:
Don't give up; I know you'll find her.

PART ONE:
Untouchables

(Jury Selection)

ONE

No one is entitled to the truth.
E. Howard Hunt

I wonder how we survived with our sanity. How we endured the isolation, the cliques, the daily dose of gut-wrenching testimony, the sight of grieving family members, the long days, and even longer nights. How we withstood not only deliberations themselves, but also the three weeks preceding them, with all the fear that their inevitable arrival entailed.

Once deliberations arrived, the emotions fell off like an old skin. All that remained was a decision.

All that remained were twelve regular, everyday people plucked from our lives like fruit from a tree. Snatched from our wives, parents, jobs, pets, and friends. Separated from newspapers, radio, telephones, and television. Wrenched from life, twelve of us sat in a room, discussing murder and madness and deciding the future of a fellow human being—a father, son, and brother. And in deciding that future, I wrestled with one simple question: *Did I have the strength to orphan two children and send a man to prison for the rest of his life?*

I have several core values, and one of them is my strong belief in the inherent goodness of people. People are good, and if someone does something wrong, it's because of something out of their control—something from deep in the recesses of long-departed nightmares. It is always the drunken father, the abusive uncle, or the neglectful mother that is to blame when people turn evil.

But sometimes it doesn't really take all that. Sometimes there is no one else to blame, no hidden entity at all. Sometimes there is just a mean person who doesn't give a shit.

I have always had a hard time believing that there are such people out there. I never thought I'd have to look someone in the eye, day after day, and make the call on whether he's one of them. This call was a big one, and the decision would last forever. It would affect not just this one man, but his family and children as well.

From day one I knew. I knew I was not going to leave this experience the same person I was when I came in. I had no idea how I would change, because the fear I felt was only partially based on this experience. It was the *decision* that held the significance. It was the verdict that bore the weight and decided how this man, his family, his children, and I would live the rest of our lives.

Like the ripple of an explosion that extends far beyond its base and uncompromisingly envelopes more of the world within its midst, the fate of one man truly affects the fate of us all. What starts as the tiniest, barely perceptible ripple can change the world forever.

For almost three straight weeks, this monumental judgment consumed my waking and sleeping hours. And I was but one of a room full of people cut off from our worlds and our families, with the burden of the gravest decision most of us would ever face bearing down upon our souls.

Those three weeks were now over and they took with them circumstance and suggestion, innuendo and inference, hint and allegation. Only we remained. Twelve jurors in a tiny room.

Searching for the truth.

Two

My name is Brian. I am thirty-six years old and have, all in all, lived a pretty great life for which I am exceedingly thankful. I have a loving family that, despite the normal obstacles that plague all four-person households, manages to stay close and caring. My parents have lived in Baltimore for twenty-five years, since I was eight. My brother, his wife, and their children live outside of Oakland, California.

I share a home with my wife of ten years, Lynne, who to this day remains my best friend, and our new baby, Kaiya. We live in a 1924 bungalow a couple miles from downtown Madison, Wisconsin. We have great friends, nice neighbors, two adorable mutts, and good jobs. We both have advanced degrees and have been public servants for most of our working lives. I help people find jobs and Lynne provides legal assistance to people affected by HIV/AIDS. We are active in our community, but of course, we could do more. We could all do more.

We love to travel and have been fortunate enough to have the resources and health to do so. We've been very lucky, and we have a deep appreciation for all the joy and wonder life has tossed in our direction.

The following is the true story of my experience as a juror on the Dan Kutz murder trial, over four years ago. I kept a journal during the trial and wrote in it every evening. Those notes are transcribed here. The rest is from memory alone, and it is not perfect. I am sure that I've missed a date, mistaken a name, or even assigned testimony to the wrong person. But this story is not about those details, although they are important. This story is an account of the events as they unfolded, the feelings and emotions that coursed like a roller coaster through my veins, and one of the most amazing, life-altering journeys I have ever navigated.

A journey for the truth. It began in early December 2000, in Madison, Wisconsin.

I have been called for jury duty three times in my life. Each of the three times, I received the summons after I'd moved to another state. With a postal change of address label firmly affixed, I received the summons notices at least a week after the date on which I was to have appeared. I'm probably wanted in each of those states, but one would hope my debt to society has now been completely satisfied.

This was the first time I was still living in the state when I was called; I was to appear the week of December 4, 2000. I contacted the clerk's office to inform them that I would be in Venezuela on vacation and would not be able to appear. I submitted my request in writing and hoped that the clerk's office would accept it as legitimate.

I didn't know if denial was a possibility, but I certainly hoped not, because I *was* going to Venezuela and there was no way I would be appearing. I was willing to face the less-than-pleasant possibility that I might soon be wanted in *four* states. Anyway, I sent it in and completely forgot about it. Upon returning from Venezuela, I found that my request had thankfully been accepted and my new appearance date would be January 5, 2001.

Sunday night, January 4th, Lynne and I were watching the local news, which we probably do only two or three times a month. It is interesting to note (looking back on it) that eschewing the local news is an extremely effective strategy for remaining ignorant about, well, local news, and thus exponentially enhancing one's likelihood of being chosen for jury duty. If I had only known back then what I know now.

The lead story was about jury selection beginning the next morning in the Kutz murder trial. Lynne and I looked at each other with disbelief, wondering if it was possible that this was the case to which I would be assigned. I had never appeared for jury duty before and had never seen a story on the news about jury selection beginning the next day, a combination of circumstances that, like rapidly-forming storm clouds, should have been sufficient to grab my attention. However, I was juror number 175. Though I wasn't sure what that meant, I assumed they started with number one and went in order and there was no way that they would get to me. Not a chance.

My second thought was, "The *who* murder trial?" I racked my brain, searching for some snippet of memory that could regurgitate even a crumpled wad of information relating to this case. I came up empty. I simply had no knowledge about it.

Lynne is an attorney, so the concept of me appearing for a murder trial sparked some great conversation. In our seven years together, we had never been apart for more than four days at a time. We talked that night about the possibility of me being chosen for jury duty for a murder trial and how exciting—frightening, but exciting—the whole thing was. How strange it would be to be apart for a few days or however long this thing took. Of course, it was just a game then; we truly didn't believe this would be my case or, if it were, that I had any real chance of being selected.

The next morning at eight, I arrived at the City County Building in downtown Madison, reported to the assigned room, and found myself at the end of a very long line. When it was finally my turn, I gave my name and checked in. When my newspaper was confiscated, I began to realize the magnitude of what was happening. I walked to the left around a dividing wall and faced a gigantic room. I could immediately tell that this was the room in which the City Council and County Board held their meetings. There was a large desk on a raised platform in the front of the room, towering above dozens of individual desks with very comfortable-looking chairs. These, of course, were all taken. In the front corner of each side of the room, facing outward, were clusters of attached chairs, seven chairs wide and six rows deep. The rest of the large room spread out around these fixtures. In every crack of empty space, a folding chair had been set up.

Almost every seat was full, with more than two hundred people in the room already, and more pouring in behind me. I couldn't believe it. I found a seat somewhere in the deep recesses of the room and waited, looking around at the sea of people. It wasn't long before Judge Stuart Schwartz came in and had us take the juror's oath. He told us that we were in the jury pool for the Dan Kutz murder trial. According to the judge, the trial would likely take three weeks and we would be sequestered, whatever that meant.

My eyes grew wide at the prospect of such a long period of time. Three weeks? Were they crazy? How could anyone take three weeks off work? I had a very flexible supervisor, but I knew that I would not be able to take three weeks off. Luckily, chances were slim that I would have to do so. But sixteen people (twelve jurors and four alternates) *would* be chosen, and it seemed incredibly unreasonable to expect to find sixteen people who could endure such a significant commitment. As I pondered the magnitude of this situation, each of us received a questionnaire to fill out and hand in. We were to report back four hours later, after the judge and attorneys reviewed our responses.

I may not watch the local news, but I do read the paper every day. My attention, however, is on national and world news. I see the headlines for local murder cases but seldom read the articles. I knew absolutely nothing about this case. I didn't even know the defendant's first name was Dan.

The questionnaire focused on what we knew:

"Do you have an opinion about Kutz's guilt or innocence?" No, I did not.

"If you do have an opinion, can you set it aside and be impartial?" I didn't have to answer that one.

"Do you have an opinion as to whether or not Beth Kutz is dead?" It's a murder trial, so yes, I do. If she's not dead, it doesn't really seem to make sense that this man should be charged with murder. What is this, a trick question to weed out the morons? I answered "Yes."

Six full pages of witness names. *"Do you know any of the witnesses?"* No, I did not, but there were a lot of witnesses. I could not fathom the notion of so many people being called up to testify in front of this jury.

Once I finished the questionnaire, I went back to work for four hours. I told everyone there that I was in the jury pool for a sequestered murder trial and that it could take three weeks. "Not to worry," I said, "I'm number 175 and they'll never get that high." I returned to the courthouse at 1 p.m., found a seat, and waited about forty-five minutes until the judge, the attorneys, and some guy who must have been the defendant walked through the door.

I looked at the defendant. He was of medium build, about 5'10" with wavy brown hair and a furrowed forehead. He didn't look evil; he looked like the guy down the street. I stared at him, trying to get a glimpse of his eyes, but I never really got a good clean view. I wondered what was going through his head right then, knowing that three hundred people were sitting in a room, torn from their lives, because of him. I couldn't imagine what he must be thinking, knowing that of those three hundred, sixteen would be chosen and entrusted to decide how he would spend the rest of his life.

Such considerations were overpowering, almost too much to comprehend. I pondered his emotions, his thoughts, and wondered if he was embarrassed or proud, confident or scared. I was at once resoundingly grateful that I was not this man.

The judge called out about eighty names. Those named were asked to stand. As each name was read, my heart skipped a beat. Did I want to be called or not? Were these people going to be released, or were the rest of us? Did I want to go home right now or stay longer? A million conflicting thoughts raced through my head as each of the names echoed through the chamber.

I wasn't called. Those named were dismissed. After that, thirty-six more people were called and asked to take their places in the box of affixed chairs on the right side of the courtroom. That was it. I wasn't going to be a juror. I must admit feeling a twinge of disappointment, but mostly I was relieved.

The judge proceeded to question the potential jurors in the box. The rest of us (at least 150) listened with only passing interest. I was sitting next to a woman named Courtney, and she and I chatted.

The questions resonated through the immense room, working their way back to where Courtney and I sat.

"Have you served on a jury before?"

A few people had, but not for anything serious. I got the impression that if someone had served on a serious criminal trial before, he or she would have been released.

"Do you have police officers or lawyers in your family?"

Ah, better remember that one in case I get up there. "Yep, my wife is an attorney," I whispered to Courtney. Several hands went up. The judge questioned each of them, but no one was released. Having a police officer or lawyer in your family didn't seem to matter.

"Who cannot be sequestered for three weeks?"

Shockingly, very few hands went up. I thought everyone would raise their hands. The judge questioned each of those who indicated their inability; most had very legitimate reasons—one was a single mother, another with a sick father, and another who could not get off work. I couldn't believe that more hands didn't go up, that pathetic excuses weren't offered (or even legitimate excuses, such as, "What, are you crazy? I can't be away from work or home for three weeks!").

"Can you convict a man of murder even though there is no body?"

Wait a second, what? What the heck did he just ask? There's no body?! I couldn't believe it. No wonder this was such a high-profile case. I was immediately chilled by the prospect of this trial, and simultaneously embarrassed beyond words that I didn't even know that simple fact. I was equally mortified by the answer I had given to the question that asked if I had a strong opinion about whether or not Beth was dead. Looks like "yes" was the wrong answer. Oops. Well, I certainly wasn't going to be on this jury now. They were weeding out the morons, and I was far from proud to find out I was one of them. I told Courtney that I had not known that there was a missing body; she shook her head and mumbled something along the lines of, "What an idiot."

The judge's questioning continued. The query list was long and thorough. It was followed by several dozen questions by the prosecution and then even more from the defense. The process went on and on.

After all of this, which lasted several very long hours, only four jurors were dismissed. Four new jurors were called to replace them.

But this was only the beginning. The judge indicated that the attorneys were going to begin individual questioning of each of the potential jurors remaining in the box in a process I would later learn is called "*voir dire.*" The judge, attorneys, and defendant all went to a private room, and every time a new juror was to be questioned, a bailiff came, called his or her name, and escorted that person to some hidden place.

On average, it took twenty to thirty minutes per juror. The afternoon stretched to evening, and the evening stretched to night. I talked to Courtney. I did some work I'd brought with me. I looked around and pondered. I people-watched. We were dismissed for an hour to get dinner, but those in the box were provided a meal. It seemed as though they were already sequestered. The judge reminded us that we were under oath and were not to discuss the case, watch the news, or read the paper. I had a quick dinner with Lynne and returned to the courthouse. The individual questioning continued.

There were a lot of vacant seats in the front of the room, and because they looked a lot more comfortable than the old, beat-up chairs Courtney and I had been sitting in, we moved up front. It was then that I noticed Karen, a friend with whom I had done the AIDS Ride the year before, sitting in the box.

The AIDS Ride was a 500-mile bicycle ride from Minneapolis to Chicago to raise money for AIDS service organizations, prevention, and support. It remains one of the most amazing experiences of my life, and on the previous year's ride, Karen and I had become friends.

The jury box was the section of attached chairs at the front of the room to the right as you walked in. It was six rows deep. Karen was on the bottom right; the questioning had begun with the person sitting at the top left. She would be the second-to-last possible juror interviewed.

I said hello and we started talking a little bit, but the bailiffs instantly appeared to break it up: people in the box weren't allowed to talk to those outside the box (meaning me). This was the second piece of evidence that those outside the box were going to be treated differently (free dinner being the first). I started referring to us outsiders as "untouchables." So Courtney and I sat and talked about her boyfriend, my wife, school and work, parents and friends, vacations, favorite movies, and anything else that would keep us occupied as the night crawled on. Eventually, I got a rubber band and decided to shoot it at Karen. She reached out to catch it, and the games officially began.

It wasn't long before I was shooting rubber bands with at least three other people. This quickly developed into flying paper airplanes and paper footballs. The sad thing is not that I would engage in such childish behavior (this is a regular occurrence for me), but rather that 150 people had nothing better to do than be entertained by it. Everyone was laughing, clapping, and cheering when we succeeded in getting a rubber band to its intended destination. It was really quite amusing, and more importantly, it helped the time go by a little faster.

I shuddered at the thought of the judge coming in just then and seeing what we were doing. I imagined what the attorneys would think, wondering how they were going to pick an intelligent jury out of this group. But mostly, I imagined Dan Kutz walking in and seeing what a pathetic lot we were. We might soon hold his fate like one of our precious rubber bands, ready to be flung into oblivion with glee and merriment.

The rubber band games represented the very beginning of a new process I would come to master, that I would soon start referring to as "separation from reality." Dozens of us were caught up in this stressful experience, in a small room with way too many people and too many confusing, unknown possibilities staring us in the face. The quickest means to maintain sanity was to completely dissociate ourselves from this situation and travel to a different world—not an especially exciting world, mind you, but one where rubber bands flew wildly across the room. It wasn't much, but it was a lot better than thinking about murder.

Finally, around 10:30 p.m. (coincidentally concurrent to the conclusion of the local news), the judge came in and told us we could go home. I spoke with the last of the possible jurors chosen, a woman named Sheila, and found out that she was number 131. It seemed incredibly unlikely that they would get all the way up to 175 the next day, but I knew it was possible. I called Lynne and she came to pick me up.

THREE

The judge had asked us to be back in the selection room at eight the next morning. I walked in looking for Courtney and finally spotted her sitting in the back of the room with two people already next to her. Miss Popularity had found two new friends, so I found a seat a row up from her and toward the center of the room, just beside the long center aisle that divided the room in two. It wasn't long before I was talking with a small group in my area: Deb, Robin, Timmy, Steve, Stacy, and a few others.

Deb and Robin were sitting to my left, Stacy to my immediate right, and Timmy and Steve in front of us. Deb was in her mid-30s and had shoulder-length hair; she was very nice and especially friendly. Like me, she was not shy about talking to just about anyone who would listen. I liked her immediately. Robin was just in front of Deb. Also in her mid-30s, she was much more reserved than Deb, with beautiful long blond hair. She had a wonderful sense of humor and seemed to be pretty good friends with Deb. I never found out if they'd been friends before they'd walked in the door or if the simple inevitability of fate, masked as a day of jury selection, had brought them together.

At some point during the morning, I turned to my right and introduced myself to Stacy, a woman with shoulder-length brown hair, wearing a sweater and blue jeans and reading a cooking magazine. Rapport was instantaneous, though I was much more talkative than she (I usually am). We drooled over numerous recipes in her magazines and talked about how nice it would be to be cooking one of them at that very minute. I couldn't disguise the fact that I am a die-hard vegetarian, so it wasn't long before Stacy realized that if the fantasy meal were to occur at my house, we'd have to narrow our dream selections.

Steve, on the other hand, was very quiet. A junior in college, he was studying for the MCAT, which he was planning on taking in two months. He wanted to attend medical school, and I found it amusing to learn that he was a bouncer at a local bar. Deb and Robin took to Steve immediately, in an almost big-sisterly way.

There are few words that would better describe Timmy than "hilarious." Timmy was in his forties, the only family man in the group. He talked about his home in some rural town, his horses, and his ironclad plan to get three weeks off work. He wanted to be on this jury, and he wanted it badly. But if he didn't get it, it didn't matter. He wasn't going back to work for three weeks anyway; three weeks of vacation were line up either way.

It was a fun bunch. We ended up spending a very long day getting to know each other. At the beginning of the day, we wondered how they were calling people to be interviewed, and I told them I thought it was by juror number. Steve was number 135 and Stacy was 140, so if my theory was correct, we'd certainly know soon enough. (Sheila had been the last one called the previous day at 131.)

Meanwhile, my friend Karen was still in the box and getting increasingly stressed about the possibility she would be chosen. She had just gotten out of a less-than-perfect marriage and had a thirteen-year-old son home alone. I told her not to worry; there was no way they were going to choose her and leave her son alone for three weeks. I told her to be honest and she would most certainly be allowed to go home. Because she was so concerned, I checked in with her often. I was at the box with such great frequency that the bailiffs mistook me for one of the "chosen few" (the designation we "outsiders" had given those in the box). Thus, I was able to talk freely to them in spite of my "untouchable" status without being forcibly removed.

My ability to approach the box and talk with the chosen few was quickly becoming legend. Those in the box were talked to, protected, and given food. We outsiders, on the other hand, were summarily discounted and ignored. There was, therefore, noticeable awe among the "untouchables" that I had been permitted entry into this privileged and distinguished coterie. I walked between the box and my seat to the amazed stares of the crowd.

Eventually Karen, and then the final juror on the bottom right of the box just beside her, were called into *voir dire*.

About 11:45 a.m., the judge and the attorneys entered the room and called nine names, including Karen's. These nine people were sent home. Twenty-seven potential jurors had survived the cut; nine more were needed to fill out the thirty-six-seat box. Forty-three numbers separated our current position and my 175, and only nine were needed. Again, I felt pretty confident they wouldn't get to me.

When we broke for lunch, I left the building, grabbed something to eat, and stopped by my office. I still wasn't sure what I wanted to do if my number did get called. Should I try to get out of it? Should I be honest and see what happens? How should I act? What should I do? I talked to my boss at work and his boss as well, and both implied that being selected for this trial would be an exciting opportunity. That was for sure. I inferred these brief interludes as support for jury leave, so I decided I would do what felt the most natural anyway—be honest and let the chips fall where they might.

I knew I could get out of jury duty if I wanted; actually it would be relatively easy. I thought back to some of the cute excuses people in the box had come up with on the first day of selection.

One woman, a law student no less, claimed that she'd had a class with some law professor who had had such a significant impact on her that it was impossible for her to be impartial. The judge questioned her a dozen different ways, but it made no difference. I couldn't believe it; he let her go.

I remember leaning over to Courtney during this dismal exhibition and asking what the woman's name was. I wanted to make sure that I never hired this woman as an attorney. Having practically been through law school myself (supporting Lynne while she went), I harbored serious doubts as to whether this woman would even make it through. We were being asked to ante up one of the few payments society requires of us, and this woman had initiated one of the most feeble displays of nonsense I'd ever seen. I was quickly reminded why I harbor so much concern about our future as a society.

The judge asked this woman the name of the professor who had such a profound impact on her. The professor's name was Dickey. Much later, the jurors who were selected came to refer to this fine excuse as the

"Walter J. Dickey principle for jury exclusion." As wretched as it was at the time, fate had it that many of us who were selected would later wonder why we had not invoked the same pathetic strategy.

Then there was "can't judge boy," as we would later refer to him. While the previous woman won the "poorest excuse" prize, this guy won "most creative." He raised his hand, in front of all these hundreds of people, and told the judge that he couldn't judge other humans. Well, none of us was thrilled with the idea of passing judgment, trust me. The judge asked why not, and he responded confidently, "It's against my religion." When asked what religion, the young man hesitated for a second and then tentatively responded with six words, six words at which we jurors would laugh for many weeks to come, "Uh, it's a sect of Christianity." This "Christian sect" approach clearly worked… but would it work twice? And could I do it without laughing my ass off? I didn't think so.

I'm pretty creative, nevertheless. I didn't really need to borrow material from my fellow selectees and knew I could come up with my own. I envisioned myself walking into the individual questioning room and, when asked, saying that I was positive the guy was guilty and we should fry him. I know we don't have the death penalty in Wisconsin, but who cares?

Or I could do the opposite, which people who know me would deem less shocking were they to hear it uttered from my lips: "Sorry, but there is no way I can find someone guilty of murder if there is no body." No doubt, either strategy would have gotten me a one-way ticket home. But there was a big part of me that kept saying to myself, "If it were you, or a member of your family up there, you wouldn't want a jury full of people who weren't smart enough to get out of jury duty, would you?"

I knew I wouldn't, and I knew it was my responsibility, if selected, to do my part and serve on this thing. I knew I would be a good juror. I am intelligent and good at critical thinking. I would listen to the evidence, carefully weigh it, and analyze every single detail. It seemed those would be good traits of a juror.

Furthermore, I am open-minded and would allow the evidence and the testimony to lead me. So often, we have experiences and judgments that predetermine our path or direction. We think we know where we want to go, and allow ourselves to be led down that path merely because it's well-lit and comfortable. That's the easy way, for sure, but not necessarily the right way. I had no predeterminations about this case. I was completely uninformed about the case and had no judgments, hypotheses, or leanings regarding the evidence or the quality of character of the witnesses, defendant, or victim. I was ready to be led in the search for the truth. Again, these seemed like critical juror characteristics.

Additionally, I am objective and trust my ability to weigh the evidence equally and fairly, factoring out the unnecessary and the unimportant. Given the variety of presentation styles, tricks, and subtleties that would undoubtedly be invoked by the attorneys, objectivity would be an important trait.

Finally, I believe that a person is innocent until proven guilty. It was clear that a great deal of media attention had surrounded this case, despite my oblivion to it. Most people would have a difficult time coming into this without biases. I knew I would. I would give this guy as fair a shake as anyone...and though it would come back to haunt me later, I knew that was what really mattered.

I've always been attracted to new and unique experiences, and this was certainly one of them. That part of me wanted to be on this jury. I knew it then and I know it now. I have to wonder, though, what the hell I was thinking.

After lunch, conversation resumed with my untouchable neighbors, Timmy, Stacy, and Robin. Karen was gone, so I walked to the box with a little less frequency. It wasn't long before Steve and then Stacy were called. I knew they would both be added to the box and I was right. A lot of people were getting called. Once they returned from their interview, they did one of two things: they grabbed their coat and went home or they grabbed their coat and walked over to the box. The room was tense with anticipation, and we began clapping every time someone entered the box. The number of open seats slowly decreased, from nine to seven to five to two.

Other than the occasional applause, our behavior was much improved. The crowd of people present was thinning; it was clearly getting close to crunch time. There was palpable angst in the air—people were edgy. We'd been there for what seemed like months and were finally getting close to the end. Although we had a growing familiarity with the process, no one ever really knew what would happen next.

Though the end was near, its proximity did not breed comprehension. It was an odd feeling to be so close to a conclusion but not have any idea how to define or predict what it would be. And worse, despite its impending resolution, it still seemed a long way off in the distance. The next thirty minutes could have a profound impact on my life.

I walked to the front of the room and talked to a bailiff—there were three names before mine. If two out of three were selected as jurors, my name would never even be called. By this point, the whole thing had become a bizarre sort of game. It was like the last ten meters of a race, with all contestants neck and neck, and the final drama unfolding in super-slow motion.

I'm a "love humans but could do without humanity" kind of guy. The environmentalist in me can't stand the havoc that humanity has wrought upon the world. The pacifist in me can't stand the violence, war, and unnecessary killing of all species, including our own, for which humans have such an unenviable knack. But I love people, and I cherish, welcome, and seek interactions with them. The fact that I knew most of the people in the room after only two days would surprise very few who know me. Those interactions were created in a deliberate effort to develop some comfort level for all of us, myself included. We all did it in our own ways; the common element was the requirement that we see this as a big game. If we had looked inside at what really stood before us, it would have been a very somber and depressing two days.

Timmy and I had long since begun to see this thing as a lottery, and we wanted our numbers called. After two straight days of this, we wanted to know what it was like to be questioned. What questions were they asking? How was the room set up? Was Kutz in there with the attorneys? What was the mood? It was a game and we could only see one way of winning—to have our numbers called. Actually being on the jury hadn't even crossed our minds; we wanted to get in that room and have our chance. I am very competitive, and it quickly became clear that Timmy was as well. This was a contest and we viewed the calling of our numbers a sign of victory.

It was 6 p.m. We were tired; it had been a very long two days. One by one, the three names before me were called. One by one, each of them returned, grabbed their coats, and walked toward the jury box. One by one, they paused, reflected on their luck or lack thereof, depending on their perspective, and walked by the wooden boundary of the box and out into the rest of their lives. Two seats remained. A bailiff entered and called my name.

The entire place erupted in applause. I stood up and started walking toward the front of the room. It was so embarrassing. Everyone was screaming and cheering. I remember looking down at the floor and thinking, "My God, these people are all crazy."

I took about three steps before it hit me and I stopped cold. What was I doing? This wasn't a game—this was someone's life. This could be three weeks of my life. Three weeks of hell to make a life and death decision. By the fourth step I was about to faint, and I truly began to wonder how I'd been able to separate the reality and severity of this situation from the game I had been playing in my mind. This was far from the last time I'd engage in this separation from reality, and certainly not the last time I'd wonder why and how I could do it. I was stupefied at my utter lack of preparation for this moment.

How had I been able to laugh, shoot rubber bands, and make jokes? A woman was dead, her body missing. A man stood accused; in all likelihood, he was facing life in prison. Somehow, all of us had been able to detach from that reality. We'd been able to create and live very happily in our own fantasy world. I wasn't sure how we'd done it, but it scarcely mattered now.

There was no more detachment and no more games. No

more separation or alternate reality. Reality, the *only* reality, waited in a small room, just down the hall. And I was being led right into its waiting arms.

I closed my eyes, took a deep breath, and started walking.

Four

A bailiff escorted me down the hall and to the right. I passed through a doorway and down a long hall that emptied into a square room. Across the back of the room, ten chairs were organized in a semicircle. I recognized the attorneys for both sides, Dan Kutz, and the judge. There were others there, but I didn't know who they were. It was overwhelming and intimidating, so I'm not sure I would have recognized them even if I had known them.

We greeted each other, and the questioning began.

"What is your name?"

"Brian Solomon."

Judge Schwartz: "Do you remember all the questions from yesterday? Is there anything you feel we should know?"

"I remember. No, I don't think there's anything I need to comment on." Oops, I forgot to say my wife is an attorney. Whatever. It hadn't seemed to matter the previous day.

Prosecution: "What do you do for a living?"

"I'm a section chief with the Wisconsin Department of Workforce Development. It's like our state Department of Labor."

Prosecution: "Where do you live, what is your marital status, and do you have children?"

"I live in Madison, I am married, and I have no children."

Defense: "You indicate on your questionnaire that you know something about this case, have seen it in the news. Is that true?"

"I've seen headlines in the paper, but have never read the articles and really know absolutely nothing about this case."

Defense: "You indicate that you have a strong opinion about whether or not Beth Kutz is alive or dead. Is there a reason for that?"

Uh-oh, I knew this was coming. "Actually, I thought that was a trick question. I said to myself, 'Murder trial, seems likely someone is dead' and checked it off. I didn't learn until yesterday's questioning that her body had not been found."

The whole "trick question" thing got some serious laughter from the entire room (including the defendant). Given the reason we were here, it was clear that potential jurors were not the only ones who could muster the skills needed to separate from reality. I was extraordinarily embarrassed and must have looked quite flushed. When the laughter subsided, the defense attorney asked me, "Am I thus to conclude that you would change your answer given what you know now?"

"Yes," I whispered, nodding.

Judge: "Any other questions?"

Attorneys: "No."

Judge: "Okay, thank you, Mr. Solomon."

A bailiff entered as if on cue and escorted me out into the hall back toward the selection room. As we were walking, my shaking even more pronounced, I asked him what this meant. Was I in or not? He said, "You need to wait here for a minute or two. They'll call and let me know."

Standing there, beside that bailiff, was an extraordinary experience. A million thoughts ran through my head. I felt like an athlete wondering if he'd make the cut or an interviewee wondering if he'd get the job offer. It felt like I had been there for about an hour, but I know it was only about twenty seconds.

The bailiff said, "C'mon," and led me back to the jury selection room. Everyone was looking directly at me as the bailiff showed me my seat in the jury box.

It was Karen's seat. I walked over to get my bag and coat. The applause was deafening as I walked to the box, elevating myself high above the lowly status of the untouchables. It was a very strange feeling. Yes, I had really wanted to be here. All day, I'd been torn between conflicting emotions. I desired this experience and simultaneously was scared to death by it. Now I was here, in the box. I know I would have been superbly disappointed had I not made it, but now my heart thumped in my chest like a jackhammer. I looked around me and saw the same people that I'd been looking at for two full days. They looked different now. I didn't have long to appreciate it; five minutes later, Timmy was called.

Another round of applause followed when the bailiff read off his name. Now, Timmy had badly wanted to be on the jury. He'd already taken three weeks off work and thought this would be a "really cool" experience. Like me, he never believed that they would get to his number. If he hadn't been selected, he would have taken a three-week vacation.

Timmy came across as a normal, unbiased person, and the attorneys and judge were tired. Like me, he really didn't have a chance *not* to be selected, and a couple of minutes later, he walked back in and took the final chair. The final thirty-six had been chosen; I couldn't believe I was one of them. Only sixteen were going to trial though, and the attorneys still had ten strikes each. So, despite all the efforts to get us to this point, twenty people were still going to be sent home.

After thirty minutes, the judge and the attorneys finally came back in and dismissed the forty untouchables who remained. Three hundred had come in and only forty walked out. It was incredible to believe that they came so close to not having enough people. The judge said the jury selection process for this case had been the longest, most tiring, and most time-consuming one he has ever seen in all his years, and I didn't have to use much imagination to realize this was probably the truth.

Robin and Deb walked by, wished us luck, and then disappeared from my life. Suddenly, it was incredibly lonely in this room. There remained a room full of ghosts and memories. It was filled with hushed silence as the attorneys looked at the remaining thirty-six, made big Xs on their diagrams, and then looked again. The whole process took about twenty minutes, but it seemed like it took a week. We had no idea if our names were being crossed out or left in. Decisions were being made that would affect the rest of our lives, and we had no idea how we would fare.

Instinct and training were used to guide the attorneys as they did their best to determine who their allies and their enemies would be. Twenty of us would go home and have a fascinating story that might interest others for a couple of days. The other sixteen would go to a three-week sequestered prison and be swept up in circumstances that would last a lifetime.

Now that I had been selected, I didn't know what I wanted. Before, I had yearned for my number to be chosen, but that had only been a game. This was the real thing. Many of us had looked at the box for two full days as though it were filled with mystique and magic. There were a number of people who had been sitting in this box since early Monday afternoon. They must have long since resigned themselves to the fact that serving on this jury was a very real possibility. Unlike them, Timmy and I had mere minutes to think about it.

We all sat nervously and waited. The diagrams were passed back and forth between defense and prosecution. Finally, the document was handed to the judge, who started reading names. Those twenty called stood up and went home. Sixteen of us were left in the box. My heart pounded in my chest, but it scarcely mattered now. It was official.

I was going to be off work for three weeks.

I was going to be a juror on the Dan Kutz murder trial.

I was going to be sequestered.

FIVE

"Few things can help an individual more than to place responsibility on him, and to let him know that you trust him."
Booker T. Washington

Sixteen jurors had been chosen to decide a man's fate. The impact of that came crashing down on me again; it still felt like I'd had so little time to prepare myself. Some jurors had been in the box since the beginning and I hoped that they'd had time to mentally prepare themselves. I just hadn't had the time. Neither had Timmy. For the "untouchables," it had been a game until we actually sat in the box.

The sixteen of us walked into the jury room, a place that would become near and dear to our hearts over the next three weeks, and Tom, the bailiff, began telling us what we could expect. Tall and very broad, Tom was an intimidating-looking man. He'd been around the jury selection room for the last two days, but primarily with the judge. It was clear that he was among the more important bailiffs here and, though serious, was soft-spoken, articulate, and kind.

No telephones. No computers. No newspapers. No contact with the outside world. It suddenly hit me what this was going to be like. I'd mistakenly believed I'd be able to talk to my wife regularly, call into work, even check e-mail. Alas, these expectations were so far from reality that it was almost laughable. The notion that I would be completely cut off had never, even for a second, crossed my mind. It was as shocking as if someone had thrown a bucket of freezing cold water over my head.

Tom explained that we *might* receive permission to have a ten-minute phone call, once a week, to our significant other. On speakerphone. With a bailiff watching and listening.

After this brief introduction, we were given an hour and a half to go home, pack for twenty-one days, and report to the hotel. We were told that a bailiff would be going through our entire luggage to ensure that it was all acceptable. No cell phones. No radios. No electronic equipment of any kind. No books on psychology, biology, or law. No murder mysteries or court case novels. No alcohol. The list seemed thorough, though it didn't include things like hallucinogens, which I was starting to think might be useful.

Still in a state of disbelief, I walked outside and met Lynne. I explained everything to her, though by now she knew I'd been chosen. She was stunned, too. She'd been waiting in the courthouse to bring me home and was in the hall when I was seated in the box. We talked about the *voir dire*, the process by which I had been chosen, and what it had been like. We talked about everything that we had to do in the next hour and a half to get me ready—and to get us ready for three weeks apart.

I had very little time at home, so we ordered pizza and packed. It was surreal. Lynne and I vacation a lot, but usually we have time to make lists, do laundry. None of this was to happen here. I grabbed the biggest bag I owned and threw everything I could find into it. Not owning anywhere near twenty-one pairs of underwear, I contemplated how I was going to handle that. I decided that I would just have to figure it out later… I didn't really have much of a choice.

I nearly forgot the two most important things I own—my journal and my guitar. Both would prove to be essential on this journey. Singing, playing guitar, and writing are vitally important to me, and it seemed clear that I would draw heavily on these comforts in the days and weeks to come.

I called my parents and grandparents and told them I would talk to them in three weeks. Lynne and I had been planning to go to St. Louis that weekend to visit my grandparents; I broke the news that we would not be coming.

I called my boss and left a voicemail that he must have loved receiving the next morning: "Hi Pat, this is Brian. I was chosen for jury duty, I'm really sorry. Can you please take care of my staff for the next three weeks? I've got nothing pressing, but will be unable to check in at all. Please cancel all my meetings. Call Lynne if you need to get in touch with me; she'll know how. I'm really sorry about this. See you in three weeks." At the time, I supervised fourteen people, so I'm sure he was thrilled.

I was shaking, trembling with uncertainty and confusion. Lynne is much better organized than I, but she was wondering how she was going to deal with three weeks alone and all the responsibilities we usually handle together.

Myriad thoughts raced through my mind. I was co-chair of our neighborhood transportation committee, and we had a meeting that night. Should I go and tell them I have to leave? No, there isn't time. Should I call my staff? Should I leave a voicemail saying I'd be unavailable for three weeks? How can I enter the "out of office reply" on my e-mail? I really couldn't do any of it. There just wasn't time.

I'd have to trust Lynne to take care of anything that needed doing. It was just so hard; three weeks seemed like such a *long* time to be cut off completely, especially without any time to prepare. All that time I was joking around and separating from reality, I could have been preparing for this. I hadn't, and it was all slamming down on me in rapid succession.

Finally, we grabbed everything, threw it into the car, and drove to the hotel. Lynne helped me get all my stuff upstairs to the third floor. We walked off the elevator and looked to the right. There was a barricade, beyond which a long hall unfolded toward a distant window.

The section was obviously reserved for us. There was a sign on the barricade. It read: "Sequestered Jury: Do Not Enter by Order of the Sheriff."

I looked at Lynne and gave her a hug and kiss goodbye. We'd been married for almost seven years and had never spent more than a couple nights away from each other. This was going to be very strange. I thought about all the things she would have to do alone: cooking, shopping, laundry, taking care of the dogs, paying bills—all the things that I do or we do together. This was going to be hard on Lynne, too.

Tom, the bailiff, welcomed me back and walked me to my room. He dumped all my stuff on the bed and started going through it. The most hilarious moment was when he picked up my guitar, looked inside the cavity beneath the strings, and said, "I guess this is just a normal guitar." I wanted to say, "Well, actually, it converts into a machine gun as well," but decided I probably shouldn't. Obviously, three weeks were not going to go by without me being a smart-ass, but three minutes was probably a good idea.

Tom left and I looked around my room. It was a pretty typical hotel room. Two queen-sized beds with an end table between them. A dresser with a television set. A small table in the corner. There were, however, a few small differences.

There was no telephone. It had been removed, cord and all, leaving scant evidence that it had ever been there to begin with.

A television set, fully visible, clear and centered, with all its enticement and allure, sat completely, thoroughly, and utterly nonfunctional. It was an ugly, black, useless piece of furniture—with a remote control.

I started unpacking with quivering hands. After putting all of my clothes away and arranging my shower and toiletry items, I unpacked my guitar. I decided one bed would be for sleeping and the other for music. I hid my luggage in the back corner. The window looked out on Madison's Beltline Highway, and a million riders in a million cars, all of whom drove by mindlessly, taking their freedom for granted. I envied them already.

I tentatively looked around Room 330. For better or worse, this was going to be my home for the foreseeable future.

PART TWO:

Sequestered

(The Trial)

Six

Sixteen people had been chosen to sit in judgment of Dan Kutz. Sixteen normal, everyday people from every walk of life. Sixteen people, representing a jury of his peers. Except we weren't really his peers because, as far as I knew, none of us had ever been charged with murdering our wife and hiding her corpse.

There was Blake, a very quiet, friendly man in his mid-forties who supervised facilities for a small local college. There was Steve, the twenty-two-year-old college student I'd hung out with as an untouchable for most of the second day of jury selection. There was George, a forty-year-old with a great sense of humor and a gigantic smile.

Mary was a little older, probably in her seventies, a retired history professor with a sharp wit and some wonderful stories. Mary Jo was a hilarious mother of two who took this whole thing in stride and managed to keep a smile throughout. Carrie was very nice and quiet, probably in her mid-thirties or early forties. Jodi, a kindly woman in her mid-forties, ran a senior center. Janet was about the same age and ran a flower business. Sheila worked for the state, and I had spent a lot of time on day one of jury selection talking to her and my friend Karen. Linda was young, very friendly and talkative, and worked for a research company.

James was a thirty-three-year-old law student. His father had been a police officer for thirty years, and between his law and police connections, we were very surprised he was chosen for the jury.

Stacy and Timmy were already two of my favorite people after hanging out with them on day two of jury selection as untouchables. All three of us had known, should our number be called, that we would be on this jury. All three of us had been right.

Rick was a twenty-year-old college student, a business major who played trumpet in the UW Marching Band. We'd played paper football the night before after launching rubber bands had gotten old. Rick was fun to be around and reminded me a lot of myself twelve years ago. We would become very good friends on the jury.

Jessica was a twenty-six-year-old social worker who'd been chosen early. She spent most of her time in the original jury box with her mother, who, in an incredible coincidence, had not only been called to serve on the same day, but had been chosen for the original thirty-six as well. Mom was let go before the final thirty-six were chosen; daughter was not. Quiet, smart, and very friendly, Jessica would become my closest friend over the next three weeks.

It seemed to be a good group. Everyone was intelligent and considerate. I was incredibly impressed with my fellow jurors, right from the beginning. The attorneys had done well, and I remember thinking that this jury was as much as anyone could ask for, and it seemed very clear that Dan Kutz was going to get a fair trial.

I also remember thinking, "This is my family for the next three weeks." Except you don't spend twenty-four hours a day, seven days a week, with your family.

With this family, I was about to do just that.

We were awakened early on the first morning of the rest of our lives and led down to breakfast—together, guarded, and special. We were all tired from the last two days; the nervousness and anxiety that had swept through us the night before had only allowed us to catch quick glimpses of sleep. We looked around at each other, wondering what to say and to whom we should say it. Breakfast was downstairs at the hotel. It was eaten, but not tasted.

Tom, the bailiff, led us to two vans in the parking lot, where we met Lori, our other bodyguard. Lori was what my friend Michole would call a "bunny with fangs." Though incredibly sweet and friendly, it was clear she would not hesitate to use her nightstick, pepper spray, pistol, or some grisly combination of the three, if the situation called for it. I surmised rather quickly that this would include not only anyone who tried to mess with us but, if necessary, us. She was of medium height with cropped black hair, and while she definitely intimidated me in a "fanged bunny" sort of way, I still liked her.

We drove to the courthouse and arrived in the jury room fairly early. Unsure how to act, how to behave, and what to do, we waited. Tom and Lori told us a little bit about what to expect. This was the same room in which the *voir dire* had occurred not even fifteen hours earlier. I looked around and imagined the judge, the defense, the prosecution—all still sitting there, laughing at my trick question response. It seemed so long ago.

After a while, Tom told us to line up. We got in line, ordered by juror number. Rick was up front, juror number one. The final three untouchables to join the show rounded out the picture: Stacy at fourteen, me at fifteen, and Timmy at sixteen. I wondered how many times we would stand just like this over the next three weeks. Tom gave us notebooks and told us we could use them to take whatever notes we desired (we wrote our juror number on the cover so we would know which belonged to whom). Tom opened the door and said in his deep baritone voice, "Please rise for the jury." Those words will likely put a smile on my face every time I think about them for the rest of my life.

The court did as it was told, and we were led into the courtroom for the first time.

As we walked in, we stared straight into the eyes of Bob Kaiser, first chair for the prosecution. He had done all the prosecution's questioning during jury selection. His second chair, Lyn Opelt, stood just beside him. Next to her was the chief detective on the case, Detective Searls. At the time, we didn't know either of these people—they were just two unfamiliar faces next to Bob Kaiser. There was a five-foot gap, and then a second table. The first chair for the defense was Dennis Burke. Beside him was second chair, D.D. Watson. Just past her, wearing a blank, expressionless look with which I would soon grow increasingly familiar, stood the defendant, Dan Kutz. To our right were seven rows of benches, separated by an aisle, working their way backwards from just beyond the two tables. They were full, but I had no idea with whom.

I'm not sure when it really hit me. Maybe it was when my number was called, maybe it was when I was led to the box, or maybe it was when I kissed Lynne goodbye. If that was the triple, this was the run-scoring single that brought it home. We were being led to the front of a jam-packed courtroom and there was absolutely no turning back now.

As we turned to our immediate left, we faced the real jury box. We had been told that jury selection was usually conducted in this courtroom and the selected few sat in the real jury box. We'd just had too many people, so our selection had occurred in the much larger council room.

We took our seats in order. Rick was in the top right. Jurors two through five sat to his left. Six through ten were positioned just in front of them. In the front row, against the side wall of the courtroom, was Steve. Next to him were Linda and Ellen. Finally, the three last untouchables: Stacy, me, and Timmy. Timmy and I were in the front row, on the end closest to the attorneys and defendant.

Just in front of us and to our left was the witness stand. It was attached to the "bench," which stretched away from us and curved from left to right. There sat Judge Stuart Schwartz, and beside him, his clerk. In front of the witness stand to our left sat the court reporter, ready to type every single word spoken at an incomprehensible speed of three hundred words per minute.

Judge Schwartz was a big man. He wore the traditional black robe and had very little hair. He had a soothing voice and a broad smile, which I didn't think we'd be seeing very much of over the next three weeks. "Please be seated," he said.

Confused, uncertain, and incredibly nervous, we complied. Just like that, the Dan Kutz murder trial was under way.

Seven

Judge Schwartz began by welcoming us. He warned us that this was going to be a long trial, as if we didn't already know that. He told us that the attorneys would occasionally confer and we couldn't hear what they were saying, but such conferences would not be important to our deliberations. That didn't seem likely—I couldn't imagine *anything* not being important to our deliberations.

Judge Schwartz read the jury instructions. Most were fairly obvious but all were nonetheless interesting. It was nice to know that in weighing the evidence, we were permitted to take into account matters of our "common knowledge and observations in the affairs of life." We were reminded that the defendant had the absolute constitutional right not to testify and that his decision "must not influence your verdict in any manner."

I was confident from day one of jury selection that we would never be hearing from Dan Kutz. He had a look about him that told me there was more than met the eye. Was there past criminal wrongdoing that could come out if he took the stand? Were there odd behaviors or inconsistencies that would come to light? I surmised that we would never find out.

We were reminded that we must reach a unanimous verdict in a criminal trial. I assumed that most of us were fully aware of this requirement at the time, though three weeks later I would seriously begin to question its wisdom.

We were again reminded how difficult this case was going to be, given the lack of physical evidence:

> *To warrant a finding of guilt based on circumstantial evidence, the facts necessary for conclusions sought to be established must be provided by competent evidence beyond a reasonable doubt and these facts must be consistent with each other and with the guilt of the defendant and the circumstances must lead you to conclude beyond a reasonable doubt that the accused committed the offense. The defendant must be found not guilty unless no other conclusion fairly and reasonably grows out of all the evidence.*

Lyn Opelt, second chair for the prosecution, rose to offer her opening statement. She spoke of Beth Kutz, her relationships with the people she knew and her family members, and her relationship with the accused. Ms. Opelt gave a dozen reasons that Beth Kutz had not, *could not,* have disappeared on her own. The majority of these related to the fact that she loved her family and friends and was a devoted mother. Opelt spoke of the growing tension between Dan and Beth and offered another dozen reasons why he was the one who killed Beth. It was an effective opening that very quickly brought home the severity of this case and, more importantly, the realization that these were real people and this was going to be very difficult. Opelt concluded her introduction to the jury by saying that Beth Kutz was dead, Dan killed her, and that there really was no other possible alternative.

From what we heard, it certainly sounded like she was right.

D.D. Watson, second chair for the defense, arose to begin her opening. Her first words, undoubtedly rehearsed in her mind a million times for this very moment, were quite inauspicious. "Death, er, I mean, Beth...." Fortunately, Watson improved. She spoke of sightings of Beth's vehicle all over town. She spoke of Dan and the fact that he wouldn't want to hurt Beth. She raised as many questions as she could, trying to steer us toward reasonable doubt. There were unanswered questions and gaps in the picture that Ms. Opelt painted for us.

Then, she sweetened the proceedings by shaking a couple grains of guilt upon us. Ms. Watson was kind enough to remind us that Jennifer and Jacob, Dan and Beth's two young children, had already lost their mother. She asked us to please consider very carefully the damage that would be wrought upon them were we also to take away their father. It was an interesting twist that seemed to demonstrate the defense's uncertainty that reasonable doubt could stand on its own. The guilt seemed a desperate plea, a harbinger of troubles that lay ahead for the defense.

Opening statements concluded. They were vastly different from what I'd expected, given a lifetime of watching courtroom dramas. They definitely maintained an emotional edge, but they focused primarily on facts. They were much longer than what could be squeezed into a two-hour movie. I was left with a mental jumble. Facts were presented and then trumped, and I had no way of knowing who was bluffing and who held the cards. I hoped testimony would give me the clues to decipher which was which.

It seemed the trial would now begin. I had been expecting high drama; instead, Judge Schwartz said in a completely unemotional, monotone, baritone voice:

"The prosecution may call its first witness."

The prosecution responded with the same lack of interest, as if this were just another day. "The state calls Ellen Maier."

A woman I'd never seen before walked through the back door and was led by Bob Kaiser along the right side of the courtroom, just to our right, and then in front of us. She walked across the space before us and stood face to face with the clerk of the court.

"Please raise your right hand." The woman did so. "Please state your name."

"Ellen Maier."

"Do you swear or affirm to tell the truth, the whole truth, and nothing but the truth?"

"I do."

The woman was middle-aged. She looked tired, scared, angry, and incomprehensibly sad. I knew right away that the woman who stood and then sat less than ten feet from me was Beth Kutz's mother.

"Ellen, can you identify Exhibit One?"

We assumed that Ellen Maier was looking at the same thing that we were. She had a photo album on the table before her and we had a screen in front of us. What we saw on the screen was a petite woman in her late twenties or so, with shoulder-length curly brown hair and an innocent smile. She looked like your sister, cousin, or a friend down the street. She looked friendly, and she looked alive.

"Yes, that is my daughter, Beth."

Immediately, Dennis Burke's voice rang out, "Defense stipulates that the witness can identify Beth Kutz."

The judge said, "So noted," and the picture was so quickly removed from the screen that we'd barely had enough time to even get a glimpse of her, much less to get a feel for who the woman—Beth—was or had been. In almost three weeks of trial, those ten seconds would be the only time we would see a picture of Beth. The defense, through its consistent and immediate stipulations, would see to that. It was the first of their constant, and understandable, desire to prevent us from thinking of Beth as a real person.

Meanwhile, Ellen Maier held her hand in front of her mouth and stifled the first of what would become many cries.

Bob Kaiser, Jr., Assistant District Attorney for Dane County, Wisconsin, began questioning Ms. Meier. It was like the two of them were old friends, and Kaiser was tightly knotted in the angst of what he was forcing Ellen Maier to do. He sympathized with her, and that made us sympathize as well. He moved very slowly and effectively, using every iota of the heavy emotion that surrounded us like a wet blanket.

He asked about her daughter, Beth. Ellen talked about what a good person Beth was, how hard she worked, and how much she loved her family. She talked about how much Beth loved her children, Jacob and Jennifer. She talked about Beth's friends. She talked about birthdays, school events, holidays, and how Ellen, the children, Beth, and the rest of the family would always spend those times together.

Ellen Maier was a very credible witness. Bob Kaiser was very deliberate in the questions he asked. Each one, by itself, didn't amount to much. But when you considered them together, it really took no time at all to realize that, despite all the uncertainty revolving around us, this woman was absolutely convinced that her daughter had not disappeared of her own accord. It also was clear that this woman loved her daughter and had nothing to do with Beth's disappearance. Her words quickly became our words, her pain quickly became our pain. I trusted her completely.

Due to the unusual nature of this murder case, the prosecution couldn't simply focus on Dan as the culprit; they had to first show that something terrible had happened to Beth, to demonstrate beyond a reasonable doubt that Beth was in fact dead. The intricacies and difficulties of the no-body murder trial were becoming readily apparent. Kaiser manipulated his way through this course masterfully, asking pertinent questions related to Beth as a person and to her relationship with Dan.

To make things easier for him, Ellen had kept a journal. One could almost smell the joy in Kaiser's tone as he asked her to read from it. It was as if he were announcing to us, "I am so pleased that Ellen followed rule number one in the 'How to Solidify Yourself as a Star Witness for the Prosecution Guidebook'." She read extensively from her journal, involving us deeply in the drama that had enveloped her family the previous summer. Although writing in the journal was clearly an established habit, Ellen Maier had not written a word in it since July 27, 2000, the day her daughter had disappeared without a trace.

The prosecution continued to question Ellen about the family. We learned about Beth's two children, Jacob (seven years old) and Jennifer (ten years old). We learned about Beth's father, Tom, and stepfather, Vern. We learned about Beth's brothers, Greg and Dave, and her friends, Kitsie, Diane, and Kim. In a flawless example of irony, the prosecution was bringing Beth to life, to prove to us that she was indeed dead.

We continued to learn a great deal about Beth herself. Each piece of information we absorbed made Beth that much more familiar and real to us. We'd started with a name, advanced to a quick picture, and now the traced outlines were being filled with all the rich and dynamic colors that make up a life. A young and vibrant woman and mother was taking shape before our eyes.

It was becoming increasingly difficult to bear.

Every few minutes, especially during moments of silence when the attorneys were considering what to ask next, Ellen Maier would stare directly into Dan Kutz's eyes with the most intense glare of hatred and anger I have ever seen. And reacting in a way of which his defense attorneys could not have approved, Dan would often stare right back at her. It was immediately clear that there was no love lost between these two. Ellen testified that she did not hate Dan, but her eyes said something different. I had no reason to doubt her testimony, so the look in those eyes asked one simple question: "What have you done with my daughter?"

I wasn't feeling particularly proud to be privy to such captivating drama.

We next learned about Dan and the way he treated Beth. We learned about the escalating violence and Beth's increasing fear. We heard about things the children said, the times they cried, and the stories Beth told.

Beth and her mom worked at Demco, a distribution center in DeForest, Wisconsin. Beth had worked in shipping and receiving and Ellen in another department. Beth had been at this job for about eleven years; Ellen had started only recently.

There was a great deal of trouble in Beth and Dan's marriage. Ellen had never thought much of Dan, but testified that she'd never encouraged Beth to leave him. Beth did, nonetheless, file for divorce in 1997. She'd been having an affair and had decided to divorce Dan. Through a bizarre twist of fate that may have culminated in this trial, he had somehow convinced her to drop the divorce and try to make their marriage work.

I started thinking about how it felt to learn so much about complete strangers. It was like being forced to eavesdrop with the knowledge that I would later be quizzed by those on whom I was eavesdropping. It was private, personal information, and I felt like some kind of deranged stalker, taking it all in.

As Ellen progressed through the chronology of the recent past, things began to get worse. There were more problems and pressures on the marriage. Beth had met another man, Greg Stahl, at Demco. The two were close friends and then became more. Eventually, Beth again tired of Dan and decided to leave him and the marriage.

It was strange—Beth clearly didn't come across as the perfect person, but somehow our sympathy was still with her. It must have been some combination of the questions Kaiser asked, the way he asked them, and how Ellen Maier answered. The loss and pain were obvious, and the sympathy and sorrow I felt completely overwhelmed Beth's imperfections into meaningless rubbish.

Most recently, Beth, Dan, and their children had been living at a house owned by Vern Maier on Highway J (soon to be simply referred to as "the house on J"). The house was in Columbia County, which is just north of Dane County.

Dan was unemployed but had purchased two pieces of property, an 80-acre lot and a 180-acre lot near their home. Dan did not work the land, and Ellen testified that she didn't really know what he did with his days. She did talk about "the hill," a particular place on the 180-acre property where the family hung out, picnicked, and flew kites.

I could almost see them: Dan Kutz laughing with Jacob as they flew a kite, his daughter Jennifer picking dandelions, and Beth smiling as she unpacked lunch. The image quickly turned sour as I thought about where they were now. So much wasted time. The universe throws enough suffering at us, I can barely stand the thought of people creating so much of their own and bathing their two young children in it. It seemed important as a juror to be able to put myself into their world, to live there and experience it from their perspective. It seemed like a critical strategy in gaining the insights I thought that I'd need. But I found it a terribly difficult thing to do, and I struggled with the taste it left in my mouth.

Ellen continued to tell us about how important this land was to Dan, despite Beth and her family's continuing efforts to have him sell it because they had so little money. He adamantly refused to sell, and eventually Beth and Dan fell behind on payments. Ellen testified that Dan was growing increasingly agitated over the land

and was putting a great deal of pressure on Beth to quit her job at Demco and cash in her retirement savings so they could make payments on the land. Ellen testified that Beth refused to do so because the job provided her family's only health insurance.

By early summer, things had started to get very intense. Ellen testified that Dan had said, "They are going to bury the four of us on the hill." He was increasingly insistent about the importance of the land. One afternoon, out of anger, Dan locked Beth inside the bathroom and would not let her out. Beth crawled through the window to escape, banging and bruising her elbow along the way.

Seven days before her disappearance, on July 20, 2000, Beth requested a "keep the peace" officer (basically, a bodyguard just in case something happened), grabbed some things from the house on J, and with Jennifer and Jacob in tow, moved in with Ellen and Vern. Beth's friend Diane was going on vacation, so she let Beth borrow her car, a green Jeep Cherokee with personalized license plates "DIDIS." These seemingly unimportant license plates would later become one of the most central pieces of evidence in the entire case.

It was fascinating to me how many details were thrown at us. I later guessed it was because certain things reverberated with certain jurors. That became especially clear during deliberations. Another reason is that the attorneys really don't know how things are going to unfold with cross examination, new witnesses, unexpected testimony, or countless other contingencies. They had to get in every detail right up front. On some level, this strategy made sense, but from my perspective, all it did was overwhelm. There was just too much information, and I found myself already having a hard time keeping track of it. How was I supposed to know which of the curve balls being hurled was the one I should catch? These proceedings had only just begun and already I was tired and lost.

During the week of July 20th, Beth seemed to be doing fairly well. She hung out with her brothers, her family, and her new friend, Greg Stahl. She washed the Jeep in the front yard. She talked to Dan on the phone a couple of times, but most conversations ended with her in tears. Ellen Maier had heard Beth's end of many of these conversations and testified to Beth's reactions.

Ellen had taken Beth to the courthouse to obtain a restraining order against Dan. Between screaming matches in parking lots and Dan following Beth to work, it certainly seemed justified. Ellen waited outside while Beth went in and emerged, some time later, without the order. Beth had told her mother that she'd been told she needed proof of abuse. A witness would later testify that there was no way anyone would have said that. We would never learn why Beth did not obtain that restraining order—it was one of many important questions that would never get answered.

Beth and her mother also visited an attorney, Todd Bennett, to discuss separation, divorce, and custody of the children. She gave her mother three $100 bills for safekeeping. We were shown an exhibit of a picture of the three bills, which Ellen still kept to this day, six months later. You could see in Ellen's eyes that there was something significant about those bills—not to the case, but to her. Perhaps it was the last thing she ever received from her daughter, and I could understand the power behind that.

As enjoyable as the week of July 20th was, things were far from perfect. Dan was looking for Beth in the parking lot at work, and Ellen testified that Beth was changing her work hours in order to elude him.

Ellen only worked until 1 p.m. each day, and then would drive to Kitsie's (Beth's friend and part-time babysitter) to pick up Jennifer and Jacob and take care of them until Beth got home at 4 p.m. On July 27th, the day Beth disappeared, Ellen wanted to get some things done around the house, so Beth asked Kitsie if she could watch the kids for an extra couple of hours. Kitsie agreed, and Beth was planning on picking them up when she got off at 3:30.

As Ellen Maier rounded out her testimony and began detailing the final hours of the last day she would ever spend with her daughter, the tears began flowing more rapidly. This woman loved her daughter, and it was torturous to watch her relive those final minutes in front of one hundred people, only an arm's reach from sixteen people who would decide whether or not she got justice. It was agonizing, and I began to separate from reality. This had to be a made-for-television movie I was watching from my couch at home. It had to be, because if this was real, if this woman was really sitting so close to me and bringing back to life this terrible day, then I would have no choice but to cry, shake Dan Kutz until he blurted out the truth, and hug this grieving mother and tell her again and again that everything will be alright. If this were truly real, I felt I would probably go insane. This was just too much to watch, listen to, and be a part of.

There was, however, no escape. I closed my eyes and I was there. It was July 27, 2000. Ellen Maier was driving Jennifer and Jacob to Kitsie's in the morning. They drove right past Dan. Jennifer said, "Hey, Grandma, there's Dad." The kids waved to their father, but he drove right by them without noticing. Ellen testified that she was concerned something was wrong at that point; it was not hard for me to see why. Later that morning, she talked to Beth at work and Beth paid her for babysitting (we learned that Beth also paid rent for the house on J, where her family had lived until a week previous, though only Dan continued to reside there).

Ellen left work at 1 p.m. and went home to work around the house as planned. At 3:30, Beth called and asked her mother if she would drive to Kitsie's with her to get the children; she was scared to go alone. Ellen Maier agreed.

As she testified about this phone call, Ellen began to shake. Her hands were trembling and her mouth quivering. It horrified me to see this woman put through the agony of reliving this moment. It was clear that she had already relived it a thousand times and was looking forward to a lifetime of living it a thousand more. The end of her testimony was nearing, and we braced ourselves for the conclusion. I thought I'd been prepared, but not for this.

Beth Kutz concluded the phone call with her mother with the following words: "If I'm not home in thirty minutes, come looking for me."

Those were the last words Ellen Maier would ever hear her daughter say.

Ellen Maier had called her two sons, Greg and Dave, and her husband, Vern. She told us about the search that night, and the searches that continued every single day from that point forward. We learned about meetings with police, search crews looking everywhere, the lack of closure, the uncertainty. It was terrible to hear. My heart went out to this woman, to her family. I could not even begin to imagine what she was going through, what fresh hell each day brought her.

After a day and a half of testimony, Bob Kaiser finally asked Maier if she had seen or heard from her daughter even once since July 27, 2000, more than five months earlier. Ellen Maier held a clenched hand to the corner of her mouth, choked back a tear, and replied, "No, I haven't."

Dennis Burke was in an unenviable position. Ellen Maier came across as a caring and loving mother. I knew right away that he would have to be careful. As Burke leaned forward to begin cross-examination, I stared at the floor and hoped he wouldn't attack this woman, because I knew it would turn me against him and cloud my judgment of the facts.

For the most part, it was clear that he realized this and treaded his path delicately, but he swayed in a couple places and took out a couple of flowerbeds. My anger was starting to well up inside until I realized that this man really had no choice. The prosecution had tried to prove that Beth was dead; Burke truly had no option but to attempt to prove otherwise.

Dennis Burke started questioning Ellen about Beth's habits. He asked her about how often she bit her nails and if they bled. He asked her about her menstrual cycle. I had no idea what this line of questioning had to do with anything. Again, it might have mattered and it might not have—who knew? It was just more information, meant to edify but serving merely to overwhelm.

Burke asked about Beth's behavior and whether or not she was a responsible person. He asked if it was true that Beth, whom Ellen Maier had already testified was never late for anything, had come home late after secret rendezvous with Greg Stahl. Ellen indicated that she had. He asked about cash withdrawals and missing money. He took what I thought was a rock-solid case for the prosecution and introduced doubt—not a lot, but certainly more than a smidgen. It was a hell of a lot more doubt than I thought possible, given the testimony I'd witnessed over the last day and a half.

It probably should have made me proud that this level of discourse was unfolding. I'm always amazed by sound reason and expert analysis, and this was both. Unfortunately, it did not make me proud—it pissed me off. I wasn't here for a good courtroom drama. I wanted an impenetrable case because it would make my job easier. Doubt was *not* a good thing, because doubt obscured the truth and thus the search for truth.

Burke then tried to recast Dan Kutz in a different light and actually succeeded. He asked who watched the kids during the day while Beth worked, before she moved out and started depending on Kitsie and her mother.

"Dan did," Ellen Maier replied with disgust.

Burke reminded us that Dan did more than nothing. "Was Dan a good father?" Burke asked. "Did he come to events and parties?"

"Yes, he did," Ellen responded.

"Did the children enjoy being around him?"

"Yes."

"Did they ever act scared or frightened of him?"

"No."

And finally, "Did Dan ever hit Beth or the children?"

Ellen's face scrunched up a little, tightening at the lips and eyes. "No."

You could tell that Ellen Maier almost wished that he had. Part of me did, too, because I felt it would have made things easier for all of us. That thought disturbed me. It was clear from everything we had heard that there was abuse, even if not physical. It was hard for me, as a complete stranger, to make the jump from emotional abuse to murder, but it certainly seemed possible. As I thought about that, I was disgusted to learn that I wasn't as clear on my own definition of abuse as I thought I was. Emotional and verbal abuse are often as damaging as physical abuse, but for some reason, sitting in that courtroom and listening to what had happened, they didn't seem to be.

I couldn't believe I was actually wishing he had hit her just because it would have made my job easier. I couldn't understand what was happening to me, but it seemed that I was slowly turning into someone with whom I couldn't identify, much less like.

Burke concluded and after countless hours of grueling and painful testimony, Beth's mother was finally finished. She stepped down from the stand, slowly walked to a bench two rows behind the prosecution, and sat down. I would see her face, in that same position, every single morning for the next three weeks upon entering the courtroom. It would still be there, composed, rigid, and distant, every evening as we walked away.

EIGHT

Tom Falk, Greg Falk, and then Dave Falk (Beth's father and two brothers, respectively) were next to take the stand. Each testified about how close they were to Beth and basically repeated what Ellen Maier had said. They had spent a great deal of time searching for Beth over the last few months. It was hard to imagine what they were going through, each day hoping to find some closure to this terrible chapter of their lives.

It was clear they all loved Beth—this was a very close family. I strongly believed that none of these people had anything to do with her disappearance. And although I was growing more and more convinced that something terrible had, in fact, happened to Beth, I still was less sure than I'd been that first day of Ellen Maier's testimony, when I was absolutely positive. I had some doubts. The question was, were the doubts reasonable? Was it really possible that this woman had just run away?

Vern Maier, Ellen's husband and Beth's stepfather, took the stand. He didn't have an awful lot to say, but what he said was important. Vern was missing a shovel and a five-tine fork from his workshop at the house on J (where Dan and Beth had been living before Beth moved out). He remembered seeing the tools in early spring, but not in September, when he needed them for autumn chores.

Vern also testified that he had been standing outside his workshop sometime in early summer when Dan and Beth were arguing. The workshop was about twenty-five feet from the edge of the house on J. He'd overheard much of the argument and heard Dan say, "If you leave me, you'll never see your children again."

This was the second time we'd heard testimony regarding a threat Dan had made to Beth. Neither was a direct threat and they could have meant other things, but they were nonetheless powerful and extremely frightening.

During cross-examination, Burke got Vern to admit that he had not looked for the equipment over the summer, so there was no way to know for sure when it had disappeared. Vern also admitted that the conversation he overheard was probably in April, and thus it would have been unlikely that the windows would have been open (as he had testified) for him to overhear the conversation.

We were being given scattered facts peripherally related to each other and were expected to somehow string them together. Then, before we could even begin the process of connection, we found out that the facts were not necessarily facts but merely guesses or presumptions that could be, and often were, rebuked during cross-examination.

It was so frustrating. I looked at the judge, the attorneys, and Dan Kutz and cursed them all for putting me through this. Then I looked at Ellen Maier and remembered why this was so maddening. I wanted it to be clear-cut for her. I wanted to help her find closure, but every time the trial raised doubt, it became more difficult for me to see how I was going to help her find it.

Several more family members and friends testified next, and the defense continued to raise questions with them—about missing checks and cash, Beth herself, and whether she really was that good of a mother.

Everything was now opaque and murky. There was nothing that made me jump up and start screaming that Dan Kutz had been framed, but there was enough to make me wonder if he was guilty. There were so many questions, and the ones that I'd thought had been satisfactorily answered beyond *any* doubt were no longer enough to guarantee even *reasonable* doubt. It was like we were running in place. There was a great deal of energy being exerted, but it didn't seem to be moving us forward.

It was exceptionally frustrating because I was trying, more than anything else, to form an opinion. When deciding guilt and innocence, everything counts. Three steps forward and two steps back, and we were headed toward "guilty." Two steps forward and three steps back, and we were headed toward "not guilty." On a vast continuum of countless details that would help us make a decision, we were left immobilized.

This testimony left me in a state of utter confusion. One day earlier, I'd felt so confident that something terrible had happened to Beth. There was no doubt in my mind—Ellen Maier's testimony had seen to that. I was far from convinced that Dan was responsible, but there seemed to be absolutely no way this woman could leave her friends, family, and children of her own accord.

I had no idea what to think—I was full of so much doubt. There was still such a long way to go and so much yet to hear. I was seriously starting to wonder if I would ever feel as though I knew *anything* about this case. I felt as though I was no closer to an opinion now than I had been last week, when I'd never even heard of Dan Kutz.

My two solid, ironclad beliefs had been that Beth was a good mother and that there was no way she would have left her children. Late-night rendezvous, missing money, and wavering testimony were starting to shake those beliefs.

Perhaps I wasn't supposed to know yet. I guess that was possible, but it seemed to be little solace for the reality of what I was facing. My ability to separate from reality was growing stronger by the minute. Sometimes, the knowledge of what we faced would come swinging back into view with the force of a wrecking ball, leaving me crushed under the weight of uncertainty.

During a break on day two, I realized how truly thankful I was that the death penalty does not exist in Wisconsin. No juror should ever have to face that. This was hard enough. I could not imagine what it would be like to not know the truth and have to sentence someone to death.

I have always been an avid opponent of the death penalty, for numerous reasons: two wrongs don't make a right and the death penalty is more expensive; the system is racist, classist, and flawed to its core. Most of all, it does not serve as a deterrent to crime. There are so many logical reasons to oppose it, I can't imagine how anyone can be its proponent.

As strong as my beliefs were, they were timid compared to the rock-solid conviction that now swept over me with near-religious fervor. No one, *no one*, should ever have to face the prospect of ending another life without an absolute, one-hundred-percent certainty that the accused committed the crime with which he was charged. I never realized, until day two of the Dan Kutz murder trial, how common an occurrence that uncertainty must be.

It is an incredibly frightening, disturbing, and powerful feeling to hold the fate of a man's life in your hands.

We sixteen represented God for another man. He may be a murderer, he may not be. We *will not* know for sure by the end of this thing; that is the only certainty we face. I didn't like that. I didn't like that I had to make a decision of such unbelievable magnitude, and that the decision would be based on a supposition. I needed certainty to make this grave a decision, and it was clear that I was not going to get it.

What is reasonable doubt? There was no body. We wouldn't even know for sure that Beth was dead, much less that Dan killed her. How the hell was I not going to have doubt? How much doubt was I allowed? Should I be ten percent sure? Fifty percent? Eighty? What's "reasonable"? To send someone to prison for the rest of his life, to orphan two children—it seemed like I should be pretty damn confident. I had no idea as to whether or not I could get there.

All we had were hints and allegations, implications and inferences. All we knew was that Dan Kutz was someone's son, brother, and father. Significant lives to hold in what seemed like sixteen pairs of small, unknowing, and uncertain hands.

More and more, it seemed those lives were sliding through our grasp, like sand between our fingers.

Watching two brothers and a father agonize over the loss of their beloved sister and daughter was one of the most difficult things I have ever witnessed. The tears, for some reason, were held back, swallowed in their unrelenting pride and stubbornness. We could smell and taste the pain—it radiated overpoweringly throughout the room. It was so potent, its aura so strong, it took all of our ever-growing separation from reality skills to keep from being swallowed up by it.

For some reason, they disguised their pain and their hurt. Because as intense as it must have been, it was not their dominant emotion.

Dan Kutz had the iciest stare I had ever seen. I later decided that his attorneys had worked closely with him, ensuring that he showed no emotion whatsoever in the courtroom. Most of us also decided that he'd been on some sort of tranquilizers or sedatives. Whatever the cause, it nonetheless did not change that constant, steady, unwavering glare.

I would stare into his eyes often, sometimes for hours a day, searching for a spark, a sign, a signal. In lieu of convincing testimony, my search for truth began with his eyes. I was confident in my ability to glean something from them and wrap meaning around my discovery. I stared into his eyes and searched for some proof, for some truth, looking, hoping for a sign that said, "I may not be perfect, I may not be the best husband or father, but I'm not a killer." Or a sign that said, "Boy, I pulled one off on you guys." Either sign would have been like a beacon leading me forward from the fork at which I seemed to be immobilized.

I could find nothing there. Nothing. There was so much more *emptiness* than evil, which made it much more difficult. Evil should have been easy to spot, and it would have helped so much in deliberations. Like all else in this trial, it was clear that it would not be that simple. As hard as I searched, I could not find evil or good, only emptiness—and that wasn't going to get me anywhere. "Emptiness," perhaps, is not really the best way to describe his eyes either, because there was a quiet intelligence, deep but present, which belied his current predicament. Within the ever-furrowed forehead, the left leg ceaselessly crossed over the right, the folded hands, and the cold, hard stare, there was something I was missing, something I could not quite identify.

In contrast, I was most definitely able to identify the dominant emotion of two brothers and a father. It was as hard as stone and as pure as an untouched glacier. And unlike the hurt I knew they felt, they made no attempt to disguise it. Rising above the pain, love, and masked sadness was their unabashed and unrelenting hatred for Dan Kutz. Whether it was because they had always hated him, or it was due to recent events, I could not say. The tension was thick and my heart reached out to them.

Yet, whenever my eyes reached out to Dan Kutz, they still came up with nothing. Although I had absolutely no idea whether Dan Kutz had killed his wife last July 27th, it was very clear from the look in their eyes that Beth's family did not have a shred of doubt.

NINE

Lying in bed at the hotel on the second night of the trial, I already felt as though I'd been there for years. We jurors were almost entirely cut off from the earth. It was as though we lived in a separate world, a clear glass bubble that isolated us from the people we saw, heard, and touched. I mean everybody—the judge, the attorneys, the witnesses, everyday people on the street, and families in restaurants. I felt as though I was dreaming, running towards the people I saw but getting farther and farther away. Their voices grew quieter, developing an inexplicable quality of distance and other-worldliness. Slowly, their reality splintered off from ours and became its own distinct entity. We were at once surrounded by that entity, but still somehow completely foreign to it.

We jurors, however, were everything to each other. Once the rest of the world began to fade away, there was nothing and no one but us. Our reality was *the* reality; everyone else's was a surreal image playing out before us, like some demented movie broadcasted directly into our retinas, leaving us unable to escape it. We could reach out and touch these images, I was quite sure, but I couldn't help wondering what would have happened if we had. It almost seemed as though they would have rippled and faded, like characters in a dream. Or that our hands would have gone right through them as they slowly dematerialized and disappeared.

Outside the jury box, or "the box" as we jurors liked to call it, we lived a strange but somehow enjoyable existence. We were safe. We were surrounded by each other, with the same fears and doubts. We all shared identical sights, sounds, and experiences. There was something comforting about living the exact life of fifteen other people and knowing they were living mine.

We were guarded and protected. We were under twenty-four-hour armed guard, which protected us from anything and everything. We couldn't go to the bathroom or salad bar alone. We couldn't talk to anyone, and certainly no one was suicidal enough to try to approach us.

It was an odd feeling, having two bodyguards at all times. I could imagine what celebrities experienced, never being able to walk out in public without their entourage. I knew I wouldn't want that. There is a beauty, one I've never fully appreciated before, in being able to walk down the street alone and anonymous. We no longer knew that beauty; it had been stripped from us like the thin membrane of an onion.

In the box, this surreal separation from the "real" world was all that kept us together, kept us sane. Were we to fully appreciate the magnitude of this image—of a missing thirty-year-old, orphaned children, grieving parents, and a stern, cold widower—I would have doubted our ability to function, much less make life and death decisions. Somehow this surreal separation from reality must have come with the job, for some power unknown and unseen must have appreciated its necessity.

It was day three when I began to realize that this separation from reality was not all in my head—it was a fact. I had glimpsed this reality earlier, both from the rubber-band-flinging fest during jury selection and the laughter during *voir dire*, back when I admitted not knowing the body was missing. It wasn't until day three, though, when supposition became fact. Only semi-amusingly, it was the prosecuting attorney who drove the reality home, by confounding a witness and causing the entire courtroom to erupt in laughter.

Bob Kaiser was a very entertaining attorney. Laughing at the prosecutor's idiosyncrasies, of which there were many, was how it happened. I had never seen someone so talented, so unbelievably skilled, and so remarkably refined at confusing the hell out of anyone with whom he talked. It was a true gift.

He beguiled, befuddled, and bewildered so many of his *own* witnesses that I could scarcely keep track. It was, for some reason, delicious to watch him ask one crazy, confounding question after another. It was the rare witness that he could dismiss without prompting at least one, "Huh?"

Here are some particularly memorable examples:

On a potential hearsay objection: "It could be prejudiciously unnecessary." Maybe it's a legal term, I didn't know, but it sure sounded hilarious, and we jurors looked at each other with tight lips, trying not to cause a laughter-induced mistrial.

Kaiser: "What does she weigh?"

Male witness, with the person in question in the courtroom: "I don't know; I could get in trouble." The courtroom was practically in tears with laughter when Kaiser retorted, "I'll grant you immunity."

Kaiser: "When the defendant was walking *from* the Stop-N-Go, was he walking *away* from the Stop-N-Go?"

Kaiser: "And what is Exhibit X?"

Witness: "Pictures? I don't know."

Kaiser: "I'm sorry, that was a terrible question, let me rephrase it." Please do, for the ten-thousandth time.

Kaiser: "Please tell me what this is a picture of."

Detective, after a brief pause to ponder what the question could really mean: "It's a couch." This was obviously a skilled detective.

Kaiser: "Can you identify the object in this photograph?"

Detective: "It's, uh, a tree."

Kaiser: "Does this picture truly and accurately depict the

object you just described?" No, Bob, it shape-shifted in the last five seconds.

Witness: "Uh, yeah."

Kaiser: "And do you remember when your birthday is? Uh, well, of course you do. When is your birthday?"

Then there were the mannerisms. Kaiser would walk up to the witness stand and show an exhibit to a witness. On the way back to his table, without fail, he would perform a quick, disjointed flip of his puffed, feathered hair. Seconds later, also without fail, we would look at each other and once again draw upon all our strength to keep from bursting into laughter in the middle of the packed courtroom.

There were the brief but seemingly never-ending stares into deep space. It was clear that he was pondering. He was planning and plotting. He was strategizing. He felt no pressure or guilt at all for keeping us here for hours while he thought up the exact phrasing he desired. It was with immense respect that I watched his patience at ensuring that the question was asked just right.

"And how old did you turn on your thirtieth birthday?" It never took long for the respect to fade into a smile as he mystified yet another of his own witnesses.

Separation from reality—a reason to smile was a reason to smile, and when bathing in a pool of sadness, beggars could not be choosy.

TEN

The most wasted day of all is that during which we have not laughed.
Sebastian R. N. Chamfort

Day three of jury duty was the day that Jessica, Rick, and I became hack addicts. We lived and breathed for the hack. We *became* the hack. Never much into hacking, this was a surprising development. I had always thought it was cool and all, but I wasn't very good and that's no fun, so it never really happened for me. As a long-time soccer fan and Grateful Deadhead, one would think that it would have been a bigger part of my life. Better late than never, I guess.

There are two kinds of hackers in the world. One type gets its kicks by hacking into computer systems. Members of this group usually get arrested at some point. The other type gets its kicks literally, by kicking a tiny leather or canvas ball in the air, a couple of feet or so, and passing it to the leg of another hacker.

The goal is to prevent this little ball—or "hack"—from touching the ground. The adherents to our type of hackers can use every part of their bodies—except their hands—to achieve this goal.

Jessica whipped a hack out during the third day of the trial and Rick and I were quickly entranced by it. The following morning we hacked before we were called in to court. On break, we hacked from the second we were released to the second we were recalled for line-up. After lunch, we managed to squeeze in fifteen more minutes. We even pinched in 120 seconds before we left for dinner.

For all of the jurors, the jury room was our sanctuary. It wasn't very pretty, but it was all ours, and it was all we had. There is a door in the City County Building plastered with a "Do Not Disturb: Jury in Session" sign. It is always locked. The other side leads to a long, narrow hallway, the one I had walked down on my way to the *voir dire*. There are two rooms on each side for jury deliberations. Both rooms had been vacant of people or activity. There is a men's room a little farther down on the left and a women's room across the hall on the right. There is a water fountain right next to the women's restroom. A couple more feet down is the room where this all started, way back in *voir dire*. This large room is white, dull, and incredibly ugly. There are a couple of old, musty sofas, interspersed with cheap laminated tables, around which are fourteen uncomfortable chairs.

Within a few days of the trial's beginning, the two tables were given permanent responsibilities. The table to the left of the door became the "newspaper table." Each day, we had the prescreened and well-sliced editions of several newspapers awaiting our perusal. (Any article or story relating to our case, the law, other court cases or trials, murders or other criminal activity, or anything else of interest had been removed by our protective guardians.) The table to the right proved just the right size for a puzzle, hundreds of pieces of which would sit there for at least ten days before finally coming together.

Straight ahead was another locked door leading to the back halls of the courthouse and the judge's chambers. To the right was a door that led into our courtroom. Several times a day, on order, we would line up right there, ready to be called into the courtroom for the next session of the trial. Number one through number sixteen, always in the same position, always with the same jurors just behind us and just in front of us. Rick led the way and Timmy, the last juror chosen, brought up the rear.

To Hackman (yours truly), Hackman, Jr. (Rick), and Ms. Hackman (Jessica), as we had begun referring to ourselves, it was the smaller jury deliberation room off to the right that quickly became home to the best part of our days. We redecorated it to meet our needs and renamed it "Hackland." The table was moved into the far corner, as were all the chairs. The bathroom doors were closed (we came a little too close to a hack in the toilet a few too many times). There was not much space, but we were happy to use it all to our advantage. Walls, chairs, bulletin boards, cabinets, and even the emergency alarm button—not one was safe from our flying, uncontrollable kicks.

It was a place where, even for a few minutes, we could forget why we were here. We could relax and focus on a tiny little ball and our incessantly futile attempts to prevent it from hitting the ground.

We improved dramatically over a few days and, luckily, really enjoyed one another's company. On day five of the trial, we got our first "double hack." It was quite the moment as the little ball, tossed from Jessica's hand, bounced off Rick's leg, then mine, then Jessica's, and then each of us a second time. It is hard to articulate how exciting it was, small as it might seem. Secluded and saddened, separated from whatever reality lay outside this room, we hugged each other with glee at this amazing accomplishment. Had others been there to witness this impromptu group hug, they would have likely thought they'd just walked into recess on a playground.

There was something indescribably therapeutic and calming about the hacking. First, it was great exercise, which certainly helped alleviate stress. I would sweat and my legs would hurt. It felt great.

Second, we could think of little else when hacking. Things happen too fast when kicking a tiny ball back and forth, and we had to concentrate at all times. It meant so much to have moments, even brief moments, during which we could forget where we were and didn't have to think about the hideousness that surrounded us. The ball flew rapidly though the air and we had to be completely focused on it in order to keep it alive.

Third, and possibly most important, were the people with whom I was hacking. We had no inhibitions around each other—we were free to be who we were. We were like children in a sandbox, just being together. There was nothing to get in the way, none of the silly barriers that we adults typically erect around ourselves and force everyone else to climb over.

It's so odd how we do that, building these protective walls around us to keep everyone out—sometimes even ourselves. I know it stems from a lifetime of fears and insecurities, but I've never figured out where it gets us. I have always been one to keep my walls down, and it's gotten me into trouble many times in the past. I have been ostracized, have lost all my friends in one fell swoop, and have shed many tears. But I can't change because it is who I am, and the joys of leaving myself open far outweigh the occasional costs. It is this openness that allows love and joy to flow in and out, unrestricted. The advantages of that unrestricted flow are priceless, even if it does get you into trouble once in a while.

It is a truly rare experience when three adults—strangers—can come together feeling that way. We could hack and just enjoy being together. Every time one of us would screw something up, we would laugh so hard, sometimes to the point of bellyaches and tears. And for some magical reason, we each knew, right from the beginning, that we were laughing with each other and not at each other.

By the time this experience was over, we would have kicked the big steel cabinet where our jury notes were stored at night so many times that its cold, metallic feel would be indelibly imprinted in our memories. There would be dozens of long, shoe-sized black streaks along the walls. There would be so many dents, marks, and nicks in this room that one would scarcely be able to walk in without wondering what natural disaster had passed through.

Sadly, most of them were caused by me.

Once, we accidentally kicked the emergency help button, calling fifteen bailiffs to action, each probably wondering what was going on and where the problem was located. They never made it to our room, and we didn't hear about the massive gathering until much later, so I was kind enough to share my observation that their rapid response system needed much work. Not surprisingly, my well-intentioned suggestion for process improvement was not very well received.

The emergency button garners only second-place honors, however. By far the most amusing experience revolved around a bulletin board. We were hacking one day, and I went up high with a textbook sidekick (my *tae kwon do sensei* would have been so proud) to try to save the hack off the wall and implement a perfect pass to Rick or Jessica. This time I managed to demolish a bulletin board that was hanging on the wall. It instantly came crashing to the floor, and the metal frame that surrounded it sprang off like a startled frog from a lily pad.

Rick and Jessica were quite concerned that we might get in trouble. Having been engaged in far worse crimes, I was not the slightest bit concerned. We tried to develop a plan of action through our tears of laughter, but the metal casing would not fit around the bulletin board again. We tried to hang it up, but the metal refused to cooperate, and instead, continued to fall off and hang lifelessly.

Finally, with the door closed, I tore the whole metal casing off and folded it up into four very long and pointy sections. We hung the bulletin board back on the wall, and I convinced my co-conspirators that no one would ever know the difference. Now, what to do with the metal brackets? In a move eerily similar to the reason we were sequestered in the first place, we needed to hide the evidence.

Laughing and plotting, we focused on our trusty cabinet for which, through the countless kicks and echoed reverberations, we had developed quite an affinity. Pulling the cabinet from and then returning it to the wall against which it resided, I hid the metal casings forever behind its metallic mass.

Opening the door to the jury room, which we had closed in order to privately conduct our obstruction of justice, we continued to hack as if nothing had happened. To the bailiff that will one day find those metal casings, let me offer my apologies in advance.

It was in the main, oversized, underprivileged jury room (with the tables, puzzles, and papers) where the other jurors spent the vast majority of their non-trial, non-eating, non-hotel time. They talked, read, or worked on a puzzle. It was in Hackland where Jessica, Rick, and I would typically be found.

"They're ready."

The call would come that indicated it was time to return to the courtroom and reality. Eventually, the call would trickle back to Hackland. Sweaty, tired, and laughing uncontrollably, we would work our way up front for "line-up" and re-emerge into a completely different, and much less amusing, world.

Eleven

Early on day four, I wondered who was going to testify next. I leaned over to Timmy, which was a pretty common occurrence for us. There is a lot of empty, vacant space in trial. It is nothing like the movies, where days of testimony are squeezed into a two-hour feature. Trial is slow. Attorneys think and ponder. They check and double-check. There are many moments, whole swaths of them, where time is like a ghost town, deserted and unoccupied.

It almost seemed like a movie or a dream, sitting in my own personal chair for almost eight hours a day, mostly unable to move, speak, stretch, or anything else that any health expert would consider critical. Usually, during trial and testimony, we concentrated on the drama that was unfolding around us. But when there was dead air, we just got bored. I have never been good at enduring boredom, and it is during those occasions when I am most likely to get into trouble.

I'd smile at Rick or Jessica. Timmy and I would whisper and make fun of people. Once, with dead silence in the courtroom, Timmy and I were talking about how much weight Dan Kutz seemed to have lost since his arrest. I leaned over and whispered, "Jail has been good to him." Another time, Bob Kaiser was really digging into a witness's testimony. "Bob's on a Kaiser roll," I whispered.

There were too many times where it was nothing short of a miracle that we didn't just start laughing uncontrollably. I could already see the headline: "Jury Misbehavior Causes Mistrial; State Wonders How It Could Have Gone so Wrong in *Voir Dire*." Timmy and I were both deeply solemn about what we were witnessing, so it's hard to believe we could act this way. Our whispered conversations were infrequent, but they helped us fill the void. They also helped us separate from reality, and there were times when such separation simply had to be done.

We were, however, enormously serious on the morning of day four as we pondered who was going to testify next.

"The kids are next," Timmy said.

"You are crazy," I responded. "They aren't ready for that yet. I think they'll do something dramatic like clear the courtroom first."

"Mark my words," Timmy said, "they are next."

As the words, "You, my friend, are an idiot" were rolling off my tongue, I looked around and noticed that something strange was in fact about to happen. Kaiser and Burke were at the bench, conferring with the judge about something. It did seem a little askew from the normal procedure.

Bob Kaiser turned and walked to the back of the courtroom. He entered with a young girl, maybe ten years old.

Timmy could have gloated, but of course he was in no mood for this. We had all dreaded this moment. We had known it was coming but had wished with all our might against it. Our hopes were to remain unanswered and our worst fears were about to come true.

The young girl was adorable—she had a sweet, innocent face, long blond hair, and a nervous smile. She walked very slowly along the side of the room, as did all the witnesses, by the benches and past the prosecution. As she walked past the third row of benches, Ellen Maier rose to accompany her. The child, dressed in a sweatshirt and a pair of jeans, walked to the front of the room, stood before the clerk, raised her right hand, and affirmed that she would "tell the whole truth and nothing but the truth."

"Please state your name for the record," asked Bob Kaiser.

"Jennifer Kutz," came the soft-spoken, articulate response. I could tell right away that this beautiful young girl, who'd been unceremoniously robbed of her mother, was bright, and while nervous, looked ready to do what needed to be done.

She walked over to the witness stand and sat down. Ellen Maier sat on the step just below her. I couldn't believe what was happening. I was less than ten feet from a tiny, fragile child whose life had turned upside-down and who was now forced to sit in front of dozens of strangers and tell them all about it.

I'd seen similar scenes on television and in the movies, but of course, this was different. She was so real, so *close*. I wanted to jump out of my chair and hug her and tell her it was going to be okay, that everything was going to be all right despite the fact that she'd been without a mother for six months. I wanted to scoop her up and bring her home and raise her in a loving, caring environment where she could hopefully regain a tiny measure of the childhood that had been snatched from her.

I was scared to death. I did not want to see this child start crying while trying to recount stories about her missing mother and accused father. I didn't want her to have to choose between Mom and Dad. I didn't want to hear if she thought Daddy did something to Mommy or if he'd scared her in the past. I didn't want to see any part of this.

I wanted out of this room and off this jury. The feeling was like an internal hurricane—it swept over me with such power. I wanted to jump up and scream, "What the hell are you people doing? This is crazy! Do you realize what you are doing?" I wanted to slam my fist down and demand action. I did none of these things, of course, but sat on my hands, pursed my lips, and prepared for the worst.

It was not nearly as bad as it could have been. Jennifer testified about the bathroom incident, agreeing that Dad had locked Mom in the bathroom and Mom had hurt herself trying to get out. She agreed that her father kept a knife in the family car, a blue Chevy Cavalier. That was about it. Like I said, it could have been worse. But I didn't focus very much on what she was saying. I couldn't.

I focused on her face. She was my little sister, the girl down the street, the daughter of my best friend, a kid in the mall. She was just another kid with ice cream dripping down her smiling face. She was an average, everyday child.

But she wasn't. She came from a family in which people cheated on each other, threw telephones, and locked spouses in bathrooms. In which people said terrible things like, "You'll never see your children again." In which people called for keep-the-peace officers and considered restraining orders.

I have never been so torn apart in my life and the testimony wasn't even that bad. The testimony, however, didn't matter. What mattered was the terror that this girl had felt. And now she was without a mother. It was very possible that soon, she would also be without a father. I often wonder how life can be so cruel, and looking at Jennifer Kutz left me with more questions than answers.

Burke, wisely, was delicate in cross-examination. There was nothing of use here for the defense, and he was sage enough not to press the issue.

Jacob was still to come. A cute seven-year-old, he seemed nervous and scared. He looked in his father's direction. Then I saw Dan smile and wave, which was just about the only emotion he would show during this entire trial. Jacob confirmed most of what Jennifer said, but was less confident, less sure.

As Burke was finishing cross-examination, he asked Jacob, "You know your father still loves you?"

The prosecution screamed, "Objection!" just as Jacob answered, "Yes."

It was a cheap shot and made most jurors shake their heads in disgust. What else would Jacob say—"No"? Were we supposed to just raise our hands, declare Dan's innocence, and move on with our lives at this point, just because a father still loved his son? Please, give us a little respect. On the other hand, the prosecution's case was building, and maybe this was all the defense had left. I was wholly uninterested in being in either attorney's shoes, so I was not about to fault them too heavily for any strategy they felt would build their case.

The children were finished with their testimony. I looked at Timmy and sighed. I figured that if we were to send Dan Kutz to prison, Ellen Maier would raise these children. She seemed like a very loving mother, and I guess that didn't seem like such a terrible prospect. That glimmer of hope made me feel an iota better.

"You were right," I admitted to Timmy, "you were right."

He managed a half-smile, obviously as lost in the horror of his thoughts as I was in mine.

Walking back into the jury room, everyone seemed deeply saddened. It was obvious that what had just occurred had been hard on everyone. We were proud of the attorneys and the judge. They did what needed to be done, and other than a small, insignificant, but nonetheless inappropriate, outburst from Burke, they had minimized the damage. It could have been much worse, and we were all thankful that it had not been.

Defense Attorney Dennis Burke was quite a character. He wasn't nearly as entertaining as Bob Kaiser, but he certainly held his own. He was tall and gangly with nearly-white hair and perfectly round spectacles. He had deep, caring eyes and a powerful voice.

Like his counterpart, Bob Kaiser, he often stared into space. But instead of looking to the distance in order to collect his thoughts and prepare the perfect question, Burke looked confused. It was quite clear why he did this: to rattle the witness. It seemed to work—on us as well. Whenever I saw that look, which was quite often, I found myself questioning the testimony I had just heard.

Long ago, in jury selection, he seemed much more respectful to the needs of the potential jurors than had Kaiser or the judge. Most of us untouchables had liked him right from the start. He came across the same way in court.

In what I believed to be an amazing talent, Burke was able to ask a very mean-spirited question in a deceivingly sweet manner. These questions usually began with, "I don't understand how…" and were typically preceded by his confused look into space. The tone or the intent seldom put off the witnesses, but I am quite sure that, had I been in the chair, I would have been annoyed.

Another "bunny with fangs," Burke kept his weapons hidden and well disguised. Most witnesses did not seem to realize that they had been ravaged to pieces until after Burke had long since finished wiping the blood from his face.

A perfect example involved one of the next witnesses, an employee of Stop-N-Go, a convenience mart. She had been working on the night of July 27th, the night Beth disappeared, and had sold Dan Gatorade and beef jerky. The film from the security camera clearly depicted this woman cleaning up behind the counter. The door opened and closed several times and numerous cars pulled in and out of the parking lot outside the building.

On direct examination, Kaiser convinced us that this woman was fully able to see everything going on inside and outside the store. She testified that no car was in the parking lot when Dan walked in, meaning that he had, in fact, walked to the store.

How he got there meant nothing at that moment, but would be vital later. We were satisfied. Next witness, please.

Then Burke stepped up to the plate. He forced us to watch the video three more times, in super-slow motion. He timed each second as it moved forward in the top right-hand corner of the video. He showed us, in excruciatingly slow detail, how the woman was positioned for most of the video: bent over, sweeping the floor. On occasion, she would straighten to dump the contents of the dustpan into the trash can.

Burke got the witness to talk around herself several times, and finally moved in for the kill. In an escalating voice, head shaking back and forth and face crunched up in a do-you-think-me-an-idiot glare, he asked the witness: "Do you expect me to believe that you can watch customers, sweep the floor, and keep track of every car going in and out of the parking lot, all at the same time?"

Contradicting earlier testimony, the witness wisely replied, "No."

"Good," said Dennis Burke, "because I don't."

"Good," Timmy and I whispered to each other, contradicting *our* earlier beliefs, "because we don't either."

Like his prosecutorial counterpart, Dan Kutz' attorney was both skilled and entertaining. Here are some memorable Burke-isms:

A witness testified that Dan scowled at him in the Demco parking lot. I was thinking, "All this guy does is scowl," when Burke asked the witness, "Is Kutz scowling at you right now?" It took all our strength not to laugh; the guy shakily answered, "No."

Burke: "How do you distinguish between an SUV and a GMC?" Witness: "I don't know; I just drive it." The courtroom erupted in laughter. Burke, smiling, said, "You ask a stupid question, you get a stupid answer." Judge Schwartz quickly replied, "I don't think the answer was stupid, only the question."

Burke, to a detective: "How big a man are you?"

Burke: "I assume with that dog of yours that you walk a lot. Is that true? Are you a walkin' guy?"

Burke: "There are different surfaces on this car. The steering wheel and the window are different surfaces, right?" Law school must have been a breeze with his keen intellect.

It was all part of the character that made up the man. It was all part of the comic relief that helped sixteen jurors survive an incredibly stressful ordeal. As with many stressful ordeals in life, one can laugh or cry, and we certainly were forced to do enough of the latter.

Twelve

Lunches and dinners were exciting times among the sequestered jurors. Lunch meant four things: a much-needed break from the trial, actual exercise and semi-freedom (both in the form of a walk to and from the restaurant), an opportunity to relieve tension, and most importantly, food. Good food.

Each night, there was a menu sitting at the main table in our hotel hallway. We would choose what we wanted to eat for lunch the next day (the sky was generally the limit, thanks to Dane County taxpayers) and write said item(s) next to our juror number on another sheet of paper. By the next morning, the bailiffs already knew what we wanted to eat. Later that morning, they would fax the list to the restaurant. They truly had it down to a science.

There was joy among us jurors when the judge recessed for lunch. We would run to the bathroom, grab our coats, and hit the road. There are a plethora of really good restaurants in downtown Madison, and we were able to hit most of them. The daily walk to and from was always quite amusing. They would line us up in almost single file, with a bailiff in front and another in back. We would walk right by my office building most days, and each time it grew less and less familiar. I would see co-workers and smile, but they, too, would grow less and less familiar.

In the beginning, when I'd say hello to people I knew, Lori would be next to me in a flash, making sure nothing got out of hand. Eventually, she came to trust me, and learned that I was not going to say anything to any of them. It took a little while, but eventually the bailiffs realized that we wanted to be tampered with about as much as the bailiffs wanted us to be tampered with. With that realization came trust, and thus a smidgen of freedom.

We would arrive at the restaurant and immediately be swallowed whole by three dozen sets of staring, gaping eyes. The focus would shift from Lori's gun to our faces, from Tom's intimidating glare to our red tags. The look would quickly shift from fear to curiosity to understanding. You could see the entire transition. Our two armed guards caused the instantaneous fear reaction. It would take about five seconds for the eyes to shift to us and see they were in no immediate danger. Finally, they would spot our red "Dane County Juror" tags, realize that we must be the poor sequestered suckers on that Kutz murder trial, and their heads would nod, with the faintest glimmer of understanding.

We would continue walking, usually to an out-of-the-way room or corner area. We would sit in numerical order and lunch would be served in that very same order per our form from the previous evening. It was very well designed and exceedingly efficient. And, honestly, it was fun. We could relax, enjoy the different scenery, eat yummy food, and just *be* with each other.

Dinner, however, was a completely different animal. We were in no hurry, so there was no need for us to choose our meals ahead of time. The restaurants were chosen in advance, and it was very clear that someone really liked steak. I'm talking obsessed, devoted, religious fanaticism here. It was one steakhouse after another. For herbivores like me, that a meant salad, a baked potato, and a roll on the side. And that was it. Luckily, lunches were delicious and always had at least one animal-friendly alternative.

Upon our arrival at whichever carnivorous carcass café had been designated for the evening meal, we could expect the same type of response from the other diners that we had experienced at lunch. Twice a day, we had to endure the stares of the pitifully curious and unapologetically voyeuristic. I'd lean over to Rick and whisper, "These people need to get a life." He'd agree.

A trip to the bathroom would, of course, require an armed escort. Tom would check to make sure it was unoccupied, and then would stand guard (thankfully outside the room) while we conducted whatever business was at hand. We were allowed, at the most, two drinks with dinner (sadly, Dane County taxpayers would not accept the cost of these; we had to pay for them ourselves). Some people took advantage of them every night. Some did not.

I only drank once. It had been a hard day and I really felt like catching a buzz. Two Long Island Iced Teas certainly achieved my goal. I was entranced by my ability to quickly throw together an unspeakably demented version of Queen's "Bohemian Rhapsody" (probably a little too closely related to the case). My eyes were closed as I roared out extemporaneous lyrics at the top of my lungs. The words flowed like honey. A lyric would form and a perfect rhyme would follow. Every lyric was, of course, trial-related.

I finished and opened my eyes.

We were in a little room by ourselves, packed tightly around a table that was nowhere near big enough. Fifteen jurors sat completely immobile, staring at me with jaws agape, their faces frozen in a mixture of consternation, disbelief, and horror. I was only halfway in the hole into which I was desperately trying to squeeze my oversized body when I noticed both of our loving bailiffs, who had been eating in the main room of the restaurant, standing in the doorway, staring at me with a look of complete shock. I could just see the headline: “Long Island Iced Teas Send Kutz Juror Packing.”

I decided it would be in everyone’s best interests if I maintained sobriety for the remainder of the trial.

Thirteen

It was our first weekend, and Timmy was starting to feel extremely isolated. He had wanted so badly to be on this jury; both he and I had prayed our lottery numbers would be chosen way back on the second day of jury selection. It already seemed like a lifetime ago. Of course, we were bored and punch drunk by then, a thin veneer already forming and beginning to hang between reality and our need to entertain ourselves at whatever cost. Timmy had it all worked out—how he would handle the time off work, the family issues, his horses. By the time his number was called, the reality of the situation was probably starting to set in. Who knows, maybe it didn't really hit him until he sat down in that box—the exact same time reality came crashing down on me.

Jury selection was a common topic of conversation between Timmy and me. Throughout that day, we had known that if they got to our numbers, we were going to be chosen for this jury. We realized full well that we were normal-looking, relatively intelligent, unbiased, honest, and absolutely, profoundly, utterly, mind-numbingly ignorant about this case. By now, though, Timmy was starting to feel isolated, and I could relate—the isolation was nearly unbearable. Think about it: we were completely separated from everything we knew. Imagine being cut off from your family and friends in the blink of an eye. Your comfy pajamas, your favorite slippers. Your relaxing evenings sitting on your couch, drinking hot tea, reading the newspaper, and listening to your favorite CD. Your bed. Your pillow. Your shampoo and shower, your favorite meals. Your dogs. All of it plucked right out from under you.

We had been separated from our *lives.*

I missed Lynne and my dogs. Timmy missed his family and his horses. On this first Friday of the trial, while walking through the garage of the courthouse, Timmy commented that it was like the movie *Groundhog Day*. I agreed, amending it to *Groundhog Day in Reverse*. In the movie, Bill Murray lives February 2nd over and over, each time experiencing the day differently. Time for us, on the other hand, continued to creep forward; it was our lives, locked inside this surreptitious world, that never changed.

We awoke at 6:30 every morning. Aaron and Paula were our nighttime bodyguards. I remember thinking, "How are they going to give us a wake-up call? We don't have phones." But of course, I'd forgotten about the antiquated, but once prized and entirely essential wake-up knock.

For the sequestered jury, it is back in vogue.

The sequestered-murder-trial-early-morning-wake-up-knock may evoke the most terrible feeling in the world. Earlier in the week, I would jump out of bed and run to the door, opening it a crack and smiling a “Good morning, thank you!” to Paula. By the first weekend, those days were long gone; they already seemed like another life. It only took four days for that once-laughable behavior to be replaced with the much more appropriate pillow-over-the-head-while-rolling-over-and-whispering “Go away” strategy.

We made ourselves pretty and presentable and would then line up at the barricade, showered, dressed, and ready for our day at the office. Aaron would take eight jurors in the elevator; Paula took eight more when it returned for the next herd. We always forgot to push the damn “down” button for the elevator and usually stood there for five minutes longer than necessary.

Then we would head down to breakfast on the first floor. Aaron and Paula would scout the premises, making sure there were no jury-tamperers lurking behind closed doors, anxiously awaiting their opportunity to extract information and tell us everything going on in the media. Trust me, they were out there, *everywhere*—we had been assured of it.

Our private breakfast room was in one of the stalest, most boring hotel chain restaurants you can imagine. It was square, with windows on one side, a door that led out to the hallway, and another that led to the breakfast room, where food was served and other hotel guests sat and ate. One of our greatest thrills was arriving to our private breakfast room and finding the tables arranged differently than they had been the previous day. Change, *any change*, was actually that exciting. “I just love what they’ve done with the place,” I’d mumble to no one in particular. Pathetic.

We would line up and start marching down the food aisle, like cattle at the feed trough, while our keepers stood guard with pistols, night sticks, and pepper spray at the ready. The stares and quiet whispers were always the same.

"Trust us, folks," I always wanted to say, "we don't know any more about this case than you do."

It was the same every day. Grapefruit sections and canned fruit. Yogurt, milk, and orange and apple juice. Some boxed cereals and maybe bananas or apples. Pre-made and long-sitting pancakes, waffles, and English muffins waiting to be popped into the toaster. Always the same. Slowly, one by one, we were shepherded back into our private lounge with the rearranged tables, set aside and cleaned each morning specifically for "those special hotel guests."

After eating, we would head back upstairs for a fifteen-minute break. I would usually play guitar, silently thanking my parents for giving me this present. I was glad I had taught myself how to play and was relieved I had remembered to bring the guitar with me to this hell. Music was a release; concentrating on playing and singing completely freed my mind from that which was occurring around it. It was so therapeutic.

These brief moments of solitude I had come to treasure would fly by in an instant, and then it was back in line at the barricade. Aaron and Paula were getting ready to pack it in and head home for their night and our day. Tom and Lori, the day-shift bailiffs, would already have arrived. We all would say good morning to our day guards and good night to the night shift. Down the elevator we went in two loads, a trip usually punctuated by Timmy ringing the emergency alarm bell in a feeble and always unanswered attempt to communicate the fact that we were indeed trapped and in need of rescue.

It was cold outside and the vans were covered in icy frost. Cleaning off the vans was a collaborative effort, and our laminated juror tags that had to adorn us at all times proved to be quite useful in this regard. We hopped in, four into the minivan with Lori and twelve into the super-van with Tom. We drove to the courthouse and parked in the garage.

In two groups of eight, each with an escort, we ascended in the elevator and walked through the hall to our jury room. Each day, it was the same exact thing—as Beth Kutz's family parted to each side of the hall like the Red Sea, we passed through, not quite looking up, not quite looking down, wondering what they were thinking. Moms, dads, brothers. Uncles, aunts, friends. What must they have been hoping we would do for them?

After the trial ended for the day, it was back to the vans. We would drive to some predesignated carnivorous castle. (Again, the sequestering gods have yet to perfect the art of appeasing the vegetarian juror.) We were escorted. We endured the muffled murmurs and snooping stares. We ate. We walked back to the van, drove back to the hotel, and went to bed.

That was it, every single day. That was our *Groundhog Day in Reverse*. But time kept moving. The calendar pages kept flipping in the outside world that became more and more difficult for us to recognize. Some part of me, though, continued to believe it existed. I felt quite sure there was a world going on out there, with work, school, bills, deadlines, and commitments. These things existed, I knew, but still seemed like distant memories at best.

For us, the calendar pages did not flip. Time stood still, replaying itself over and over again, never changing. It was not like time was dead—more like it had been ripped away from us and put on display like an exhibit in a museum. We recognized it, we could see and ponder its existence, but in reality it had little bearing upon our lives. In our lives, time was a complete and total nonentity.

A *Groundhog Day in Reverse*.

Fourteen

Saturday was literally like the last day of school; anticipation about the prospect of having Sunday off grew tangibly. We needed it. But before we could get too excited, we still had another day of testimony to endure (unlike the regular world, we only got one day off a week).

One friend after another testified about what a good person, how conscientious a worker, how dedicated a mother Beth was. The testimony was very powerful and served to support my conviction that Beth would not have simply disappeared on her own. Again, given the fact there was no body, this was essential for the prosecution.

We learned about a hair appointment—Beth had come in and talked to several of her friends at the salon. They each testified that Beth was in a stressed and frightened state of mind and that Dan was waiting for her when she left. He pulled out in front of her and blocked her car so she couldn't leave. Her friends testified how Beth and Dan had argued in the street and eventually Dan had started yelling at Beth, right in front of the children.

We learned about Dan following Beth to work with increasing regularity. Numerous friends saw Dan at Demco or heard from Beth that he'd been there. It got so bad that Beth had to change her hours so Dan wouldn't know when she started and ended her workday. It hadn't seemed to work, because he was still following her.

He was checking in on her, calling her with increasing frequency. It seemed he was trying to control Beth and her activities. We learned about failed attempts to reach Beth by phone, many by people who claimed that Dan had disconnected the phone to keep Beth from talking to her lover, Greg Stahl.

We learned about Greg Stahl—a quiet, reserved man of medium build with a dark mustache. He worked at Demco and Beth had been seeing him for some time. Most friends felt that he cared about her. He testified and talked about his concern for Beth. He talked about their relationship and his desire that she leave her husband and be with him. He talked to Beth regularly at work.

On the afternoon of July 27th, Stahl noticed a change in Beth's behavior somewhere around noon. It was as if something had happened—a phone call, a visit, something—that turned her previously happy mood sour. He didn't know what it was. At one point, Stahl went on the roof of the building to see if Dan was watching Beth, and he was. Stahl walked outside just as Dan was driving by.

"Hey, buddy, why don't you get a life," Stahl screamed in Dan's open window as the car went by. Knowing what we now know, it seems like this may have been a fairly stupid thing to do. Maybe Stahl was brazen and overconfident. Maybe he really hoped it would work, and that Dan would just wise up and leave Beth alone. Maybe he was frustrated at seeing his girlfriend cry and wondered what to do about the stalker who also happened to be her husband. If indeed he loved Beth, and he very well may have, maybe it was out of a complete sense of desperation.

Stahl then called and met with a policeman about Dan being at Demco. The officer went looking but did not find him. We would later learn from that very police officer that he had gone in one direction to find Dan, but that Dan had gone in an entirely *different* direction for a very specific purpose.

Greg Stahl looked saddened by his loss. Maybe I was wrong, but I believed him. There are many characteristics to describe me, and two are pertinent in this case. Neither of these, unfortunately, adds much credibility to the value of my opinion. First, I am a sucker. I am overly optimistic, think the best of everyone, and have to be whipped over the head many times to believe otherwise. Second, I am a hopeless romantic. I believed Stahl and felt sorry for him, but other members of the jury were not as easily swayed. It was a critical opinion formed from ten minutes of testimony.

It was not as if we would get another chance to meet the man; those ten minutes were all we had. It was just one more of the crazy elements of the jury trial. We had ten minutes to meet and listen to a central character in this play and decide whether we could trust him or not. This was a decision that normally would take most people months of interaction to make. We had ten minutes and were limited to the interaction the attorneys dictated.

On cross-examination, Burke got Stahl to admit that Beth had come home late because of secret, late-night rendezvous with him.

Obviously, Burke was still trying to convince us that Beth was not as reliable as she was being portrayed, but this strategy was scoring fewer and fewer points with me. It might have worked five days before, but things were changing, and I was starting to believe that something had happened to Beth. At this point, all Burke did was convince me that Beth was not perfect, which I'd never really thought was the case in the first place. He also asked whether Beth was menstruating during their final sexual encounters. I was not sure what this had to do with the price of oranges in Oslo, but I figured we'd find out eventually.

Kitsie testified about her relationship with Beth and that she was, as we had already heard, watching the children last July 27th. Usually, Kitsie watched the kids until 1 p.m., when Ellen would pick them up. That day, however, Beth had asked her to watch them a couple hours longer. Kitsie and the kids talked to Beth several times that day and corresponded with her via e-mail.

Before leaving work, Beth had called to say she'd be coming over to get the children. It was the last time that Kitsie would ever hear her voice. Later that afternoon, when Beth had not come to get the children, Kitsie got in touch with Ellen to inquire about where Beth might be. She watched the children until later that night when Ellen and Vern were able to pick them up, long after Beth should have.

Beth seemed to have a great number of caring friends. It was very clear that not one of them felt she had taken off by choice. Like her family, Beth's friends seemed pretty convinced about what had happened.

If only I could be.

Fifteen

The first Sunday of the trial, almost a full week after the whole thing began, was visiting day. Furthermore, it was our first day off since arriving in this world. I quickly developed a new appreciation for what a prisoner feels when someone he or she loves comes to visit. We had to meet in a common area, and we had to choose a time and stick to it. We had only twenty-five minutes—twenty-five minutes that would be witnessed by other "prisoners" and their visitors, as well as our ubiquitous friends from the Dane County Sheriff's office.

It was a peculiar feeling, not having seen Lynne for almost five days. It was the longest we had ever gone without seeing each other. I really wanted to see her, but at the same time I did not. I was worried that seeing her like this, in this way, for such a short period of time, would be worse than not seeing her at all. Twenty-five minutes is not a lot of time. I knew it would be over in an instant, and I would have to say goodbye to her again. I have never been very good at goodbyes.

I was very nervous, too. I felt like a different person already and wondered if she would recognize me. It had only been four and a half days, not four and a half years, but there was something oddly puzzling about the way I felt about myself. I felt as though I was living in some surreal place outside myself, while an imaginary imposter was playing my role in a way I could have scarcely scripted. I was angry with myself but was unsure why. I figured it was because I was so nervous about seeing Lynne.

I soon discovered that there was nothing to worry about. The visit was great. I was signed up for the 4:00 p.m. time slot, along with Jessica and Mary. We were all sitting around that afternoon doing our own thing. Some were watching movies. Others were watching the NFL playoffs in the common room with Aaron. It was pretty relaxing. Every half hour, three jurors would come back upstairs looking dejected, and three more, barely able to contain their excitement, would be led down. This went on for the entire afternoon.

Finally, four o'clock rolled around and Mary, Jessica, and I met at the barricade. We were led downstairs to our breakfast room and each told to sit at a different table inside. After a few minutes, the door to the breakfast area opened and a bailiff escorted our guests in.

In came Mary's husband, Jessica's mom, and Lynne. Lynne and I hugged for two minutes. It was amazing to see her. I was pretty sure she recognized me. We sat down at a table and started talking. Lynne told me about her life on the "outside," and I talked about what it was like to be sequestered. We weren't allowed to talk about the trial at all—any mention of anything related to the trial would result in Lynne being sent directly home. I was dying to tell her everything going on in my surreal little world, but I could not.

So we talked more about her world. Dogs, bills, work, and friends. Wow, she was having a life out there! It didn't seem fair, but I was glad that she was going out with her friends, having some fun, and managing to take care of all the stuff around the house. She was still sane and surviving without me. She was, however, spending just a little too much time with our friend John. *Hmmm*, I wondered.

Listening to her voice, seeing her beautiful eyes, holding her hands...it didn't last long enough, but each of these things seemed more precious and priceless than they had in a long time. It was very good to see her. Naturally, our time was up before we knew it, and we kissed goodbye. I knew I would have to wait a full week to see her again and hoped that the brief reminder of her smile and the taste of her lips would stay with me for that long.

There was something remarkable about Sunday. One would think that an entire day sitting in one quadrant of a hotel would be boring, but when the alternative is listening to tales of murdered wives, lost mothers, and grieving families, boredom takes on an entirely different meaning. It was one magical day in which we didn't have to pay attention to every word, every mannerism, every pause and nervous tick, in some feeble but absolutely necessary attempt to judge, analyze, weigh, and theorize the credibility and importance of all that was laid before us. It was one whole day without having to see the miserable and depressed faces of strangers that we knew all too well. Strangers who were facing one of the most hideous realities imaginable. Strangers who were, unfair as it was, counting on us to make it all right.

It doesn't seem like much, but to us, a whole day stuck in the hall of some rotten hotel, with little freedom and even less excitement, was the most precious reward we could have imagined.

I went to bed with a smile on my face. It wasn't long before it disappeared into the disparaging knowledge that it would be another six days before it would return.

SIXTEEN

"Other than being sequestered, this is really cool."
Timmy, Juror #16, Dan Kutz Murder Trial

It was now Monday, exactly one week after we had reported to a gigantic room full of strangers to begin our trip down Destiny Lane. The previous Monday, I had had too much fun by sending rubber bands into the air. This Monday, one week later, I got nailed for something similar. On the one hand, it was extremely frustrating; on the other, it's amazing I made it that long. Nevertheless, I was peeved.

There seemed to be an occasional lack of understanding among our captors that we were being locked away like prisoners for three full weeks through no fault of our own. Despite our dedication to serving, it was occasionally forgotten that we had lives out there, real lives which had been suddenly silenced—not merely interrupted, but silenced—and a little bit of slack would have been nice.

Three weeks is a long, long time to have your life silenced.

I was immediately thankful that Rick, Jessica, Stacy, and Timmy were there with me. I couldn't imagine going through this without them. They were nice to be around and fun to spend time with; they made this experience palatable. This was a great bunch of jurors, but some people were certainly more fun to be around than others.

Some people connected better than others did. As unique as this experience was, it was still life; it still offered the social realities that humans experience a thousand times a day, in a thousand different situations. The problem was that those with whom I had connected were, like me, inherent troublemakers. It kept me going, but it was also the cause of my ruin. Or, perhaps, I was the cause of theirs. It certainly wouldn't have been the first time.

Yes, it was true that Jessica, Rick, and I had the most fun. Yes, it was true that we provided comic relief for the troops and for ourselves, on perhaps too regular a basis. Yes, it was true that we walked a very thin line and maybe, occasionally, blasted right over it.

On the outside, laughter and humor are some of the most important cornerstones of my existence. I like to think that I am a great storyteller, but sadly, those closest to me call me the "King of Hyperbole" instead of the "King of Stories."

"What's a little exaggeration among friends for an extra laugh?" I always ask.

On the inside, in that isolated, structured, incredibly intense and stressful environment, the importance of laughter increased one-hundred fold. Some of my co-jurors wholeheartedly agreed, some did not.

Sunday morning, before visiting hours had begun, we had gone out for breakfast at a pancake house. There are no words to describe how amazing it was to go out for breakfast and eat something, *anything*, other than that godforsaken grapefruit and those day-old cardboard pancakes. It was a nice change in routine, which by this time had become a flat-out good thing, no matter what it was.

Usually, we were tucked away in some quiet room or the corner of a restaurant when we went out, but on this occasion, we were seated at a long table right in the middle of the restaurant. We digested the typical hushed whispers and pointed fingers with our usual panache and savoir-faire. On a sunny day in January, in an over-packed, family-oriented pancake restaurant, sixteen jurors and two armed deputy sheriffs were bound to attract attention.

We were in the middle of the restaurant in broad daylight. Given our penchant for misbehaving, it was clear from the beginning that this *could* be dangerous. We were pretty good, for the most part. We *might* have made a couple of obnoxious comments. It is also *possible* that we hung our juror tags from our eyeglasses, eyebrows, and ears. I have a *vague* recollection of a paper football traveling back and forth across the table and then somehow, apparently of its own accord, leaving my fingers and flying across the restaurant and landing on the floor near another table.

Okay, I admit that we were acting a little goofy. The flying paper football was a bad idea. But really, it was not earth-shattering. And once it flew, we decided that we were standing too far over the line and it was time to stop. To our credit, we did.

Fast-forward to Monday, when Rick, Jessica and I were hacking during break in our favorite place, Hackland. Lori the bodyguard, who was normally sweet, burst in and chastised us for our loud, immature, and inappropriate behavior the day before. She then poured lemon juice into the gushing contusion she has just created by proclaiming that not one, two, or even three, but four—yes, *four*—of our fellow jurors had complained about our behavior and we had better shape it up from that point forward.

Looking back on it, it seems kind of silly, but at the time I was furious. Better "shape up" or what, they're going to send us home? Was this becoming like a season of "Survivor," in which we started forming pacts to decide which jurors should be kicked off the island?

Jessica didn't even participate in the festivities but got thrown into the "complaint" simply because she was part of the hack-pack. Maybe the other jurors were resentful because we seemed to be having too much fun. It could have been because they were jealous of the bond we had formed. Maybe it was that Rick and I were too loud and some people were annoyed by that. Either way, people were definitely starting to get a little ornery, which was understandable. But tattling on co-jurors? I couldn't help wonder why they couldn't just tell us themselves. We were all adults and, for better or worse, we were all in this together. I was disappointed.

I must admit that we *were* acting a little immature. We still had a long road to hoe, and it was important that we were able to communicate our needs with each other. In fact, given what we were facing in deliberations, it was vital. It was the first ominous harbinger of the troubles yet to come.

For me, sucking the fun out of this affair would have done little to make things better, make this endurance test any more bearable, or make the confusion and frustration we were facing any less troubling. There were precious few things helping to sustain the bridge that led back to reality, and laughter and humor, as inappropriate as they may have seemed given the circumstances, carried much of the weight.

Unfortunately, we were not sent back to the hotel for misbehaving. We were given the worst punishment of all: more testimony.

In the courtroom, we learned more about the precious 180-acre property that Dan had purchased. We learned about the hill where the family flew their kite, the price Dan had paid for the property, the importance of keeping the land and making the payments, and the fact that Dan felt the land was more important than Beth's job, despite the health benefits it provided for the children. Dan was obsessed with keeping this property. We heard it time and again from witness after witness. It was clear that he felt there was no way the family would survive without keeping the land. The problem was that they couldn't afford it and time was running out.

Payments were way behind, and the Kutz family was in no position to catch up. The bank foreclosed on the property on July 27, 1999. A one-year redemption period was granted, after which the property would be handed off for sheriff's auction. It seemed that Dan believed that he had one last chance to get the land, and that last chance fell on the one-year anniversary of the foreclosure.

Until this point, the testimony had been interesting, but not really earth-shattering. As I've mentioned, the majority of what we had heard didn't hold much weight for me and didn't seem that important. Trial has so much dead air, and a preponderance of the testimony was exactly that. It was rare that we received a piece of information that would fly like a cannonball from the mouth of the witness directly into our brains and explode on impact. That is exactly what happened when I realized what I'd just heard. It didn't seem possible that it could be a mere coincidence.

The one-year anniversary and Dan's last chance to save the property that meant the world to him fell on July 27, 2000, the day Beth Kutz disappeared without a trace.

Seventeen

Day seven of the prosecution witnesses' testimony was extraordinarily powerful. I couldn't have imagined a more effective witness than Beth's mother Ellen, but I was wrong. If Ellen was a snowball, Detective Heimerl was an avalanche.

He filled in a number of gaps, testifying about the night of July 27th. Later that night, after the search efforts for Beth came up empty, Detective Heimerl had been sent to question Dan at his brother's house.

Dan told the detective a story of reconciliation with Beth. Dan admitted that he and Beth had talked, been together, and had intercourse. Later that night, they drove to the Stop-N-Go to get some food. Dan left his boots in Beth's Jeep by accident, but nevertheless insisted on walking home from the convenience store, which would have been about twenty-five miles away. In this scenario, Beth would have said goodbye, dropped him off, and driven home alone.

That was all Dan knew about what had happened to her. He started walking home and was spotted by a Meriter nurse on her way to work, who called the police. Dan was later questioned by Officer Blake of the DeForest Police Department. Officer Blake testified that Dan was barefoot, looked dazed, and seemed as though he'd been drinking and in a car accident.

Dan told Officer Blake that he had hitched a ride to the Stop-N-Go with strangers but didn't know the make and model of the vehicle. He'd accidentally left his boots in *their* car. He asked the officer for a ride to his brother's house and was given one. He never said anything about Beth. This was a vastly different story than he would tell Heimerl later that night.

Heimerl initiated an investigation after Dan was taken into custody that night and reported several interesting findings:

- Dan's Chevy Cavalier was found at his brother John's workplace.
- John's Cougar, which Dan had borrowed on July 27th, was parked by the side of the road near Beth's workplace, past which Beth would have driven on her way home from work.
- The only key to this car was found, one week later, in the gravel driveway of the 180-acre property Dan and Beth owned.
- A witness had seen Beth in her green Jeep Cherokee entering the 180-acre property on the afternoon of July 27th.
- Beth had asked her mother to come with her to Kitsie's. She said to her, "If I'm not home in thirty minutes, come looking for me."

The coincidences, or, as they're known in the justice system, "circumstantial evidence," mounted so rapidly that it was becoming difficult to see over the top. Each item was added to the last, layering itself as a thought that became an idea, a hypothesis, a theory, and finally a truth. We barely had time to consider one item before the next layer was added.

In the early days, the evidence that would become these layers was merely being spread across the floor, like a thousand puzzle pieces thrown randomly into an empty room. There they lay in meaningless and disconnected chaos. Then, slowly, the reds began to gather themselves as flowers, the yellows as sun, the blues as sky, the greens as grass. Still intermingled and upside down, still disjointed and divided, they were scattered about with minimal rhyme and seemingly nonexistent reason. It was slow and tedious work to find any order in the chaos.

Over the last two days, however, this started to change. The pieces began to move themselves quickly to their grouping and even more quickly to their proper positions as Bob Kaiser, the sorcerer, waved his wand from the periphery. As if by magic, the picture was beginning to tell a story that made sense and became increasingly reasonable and comprehensible.

For the first time, I found myself having to make internal, semi-conscious decisions about guilt and innocence. I had to face the absolute possibility that this guy might be guilty; that Dan Kutz really did, in some crazed moment of frustration, guilt, anger, jealousy, misery, greed, and immeasurable desperation, kill Beth. It washed over me again that this was a person, a friend, and a mother about whom we were talking.

Someone I now knew well. It was hard—and it was heartbreaking. But I found myself—finally— edging closer to an opinion.

Even though I fervently hoped that Beth would walk through the doors of the courtroom with a smile, I was facing the increasing reality that this was quite unlikely. Timmy and I talked about it often in our little corner of the box. At first, he thought I was kidding and he didn't find it amusing. Then, after a while, he realized I was serious and decided he'd very much like to see the same thing: Beth would walk through the door, heal her family, and allow us all to go home.

Day after day, I sat fifteen feet from a man who might be a murderer. And though I had managed to keep that thought from surfacing too often prior to Heimerl's testimony, the prosecution brought this possibility home with the power of a giant hammer.

Detective Heimerl did not place the final nail in the coffin with his testimony about cars, keys, and changing explanations. He was, however, an incredibly powerful witness. By the time he was finished, I had to admit it was difficult to imagine how anyone would find the strength to pry the lid off a case that was inching closer to being forever sealed.

EIGHTEEN

Nights were not usually that exciting for the sequestered. We would get back home from dinner around eight, sometimes nine, and people were pretty tired. It was never long afterward that movie night began in the VCR common room.

The VCR common room was the first room on the left upon entering our barricaded hallway. In it sat a giant hot tub, which we failed to use even once, and a king-sized bed. In front of the bed was a television set that had been wired to work only with the VCR. This was the movie room, and it was common for anywhere from four to ten jurors to be cramped in here, on or around the bed or in the two thoroughly uncomfortable chairs. We grew quite close in this room, which we had creatively dubbed "the movie room."

In the room directly across the hall were our bailiffs. Whatever they were doing, the TV was *always* on. It was in this room, "the TV room," that we were allowed to view that all-powerful god of modern life, the television. It was the only functioning television set in our world. It was a simple world, comprised of an eighteen-room hallway, two vans, a jury room, a courtroom, a couple of restaurants, and a single television set.

We could watch our sole functioning TV, but only with supervision. We had to agree on the program, and certain shows were off limits. Aaron usually watched with us, Paula occasionally. Either way, we were never left to our own devices regarding the media. Aaron had an unbelievably quick trigger finger with the remote and could change the station the second a commercial break began, ensuring that we didn't catch even one brief second of a local news lead-in for that evening. Boy, he was good.

There was really only one other social area in our world. It was the far end of the hall, which dead-ended at a window overlooking the Beltline, where I would sit and play guitar. Sometimes Rick would play with me, and Jessica often hung out to listen. Several jurors would occasionally venture down to chat, listen, or sing along. It was a nice place, and it brought us together in a positive way.

Movie room, TV room, and guitar corner at the end of the hall: that pretty much summed up our hotel-based social life.

On occasion, our world ventured away from the familiar and we were permitted to do something different. One of the few examples of such was swim night.

It took a particular alignment of the stars to make a swim night happen (everything is complex in the world of the sequestered). We would begin by begging Aaron and Paula to let us go. Once they agreed, they chose a time, usually around nine. Then Aaron would slip behind the barricade to arrange the outing.

The barricade was not merely erected to keep people out; it was also the end of the earth for us jurors. It was the terminus of the safety zone, the farthest frontier of our folly. We simply could not go past it. Just beyond this barricade, several things laid in wait: an ice machine, a vending machine, and an elevator. Far beyond the elevator lay another hall with another set of rooms. Few, if any, people ever graced this area and, if they did, it was only for a moment as they quickly worked their way back to their rooms or caught the elevator back to the lobby.

Despite its complete harmlessness and general vacant, uninhabited nature, the area past the barricade remained completely off limits. We looked with longing and desire at this "free area" that existed beyond our borders, wishing that, for just a second, we could frolic freely without a bailiff at our side. Alas, not even full view of the light was enough to grant us reprieve from Plato's cave.

So we aligned ourselves at the end of our world and waited for Aaron to take us swimming. He had already gone downstairs and cleared out the pool. "Sorry kids, Mommy and Daddy have to take you back to the room now. Sequestered jury coming along." With yet another sign blocking outsiders from entering, the pool was completely secured on our behalf: a private party thrown just for us.

Paula had already walked down the hall and knocked on each door, informing jurors that "We are swimming tonight at nine, if anyone is interested."

The first time we swam, fifteen of sixteen jurors were in attendance. That was only the second night of trial, and it was like a pool party.

Imagine fifteen people who barely knew each other walking down the stairs single file with a Dane County Deputy Sheriff leading the way, all in their swim suits (except the deputy, of course). It must have been quite a sight. When we entered the pool area, we saw the smallest swimming pool in existence. It couldn't possibly have been more than thirty feet long by fifteen feet wide. I've seen bigger hot tubs. Speaking of which, the hot tub sat just to the left in the back corner of the room. To the right and through another door was the workout room. Straight ahead, along the far wall of the pool room, was a long window that ran the length of the wall, with a door that led out to a small sundeck/porch area.

That first night, at least ten of us got into the pool at the same time. Three or four of us sat along the edge, chatting, while five or six tried to swim laps. We must have looked hilarious. The pool was so narrow we had to swim right next to each other in order for us all to fit. We were so close we would whack each other with regularity. Then there was the length: I could get wall to wall in three strokes. Then I'd turn around. Six of us, doing this simultaneously.

Eventually, I got out and lifted weights for a while on the most terrible, non-functioning workout machine I had ever encountered. This exercise in futility was beyond worthless to my muscles, but it gave me a fleeting sense of normalcy. Deserved or not, it was a feeling to be treasured.

Aaron came in to the workout room with Linda, Mary, and me, with the unmistakable plan of studying the television set. We asked if we could watch something while we worked out, and I even told him he'd be able to see the set from his seat in front of the door to the pool area. He said "no" and walked out. Less than a minute later he was back, walking straight to the TV. I was so excited that he'd changed his mind, and said so.

"Aaron," I said, "we really appreciate this."

"What's that?" he asked, as he leaned forward and removed the cable from the television set to ensure that we wouldn't try to sneak even one unsupervised second.

"Nothing," I said. Remember that fleeting sense of normalcy? Scratch that thought.

Meanwhile, a bunch of jurors had settled into the hot tub. It was small, and there were lots of us (especially after I decided to join them), so this was amusing. At some point, my incredibly childish nature began to dominate yet again, and I decided it would be cute to run outside on the deck. In my swim suit. In January. In Madison, Wisconsin.

It was cold, and the ground was completely covered with about twelve inches of snow and ice. I walked right through it for a while and took in the fresh air. Then I ran back inside and jumped in the hot tub. It felt great. Rick and Timmy were right behind me, but they had to one-up me—they actually laid down in the snow and made snow angels. I thought they were insane but then the testosterone kicked in, and I flopped down beside them.

I could feel the snow melting down my back as I ran inside and jumped back into the hot tub. After twenty seconds, when feeling returned to my body and my heart started beating again, a smile inched its way across my face. Rick, Timmy, and I made several more snow angels before the night was through.

During one run back into the hot tub, I happened to catch Aaron's eye. I couldn't imagine what was going through his mind, but I sure hoped he wasn't going to share it with counsel. If I hadn't already solidified my position as the biggest, most immature, puerile juror in the history of jury duty, I had certainly now achieved that distinction. And because immaturity, like misery, loves company, I was pleased to know I was not alone.

The following morning, Tom did not report to Jury Hall. We learned that he had injured his shoulder and we had lost our chief bodyguard. We had become very fond of him and were saddened to hear the news.

We were still digesting the notion that a member of our coterie was about to be replaced when the new guy walked off the elevator and into our lives. His name was Kurt. We were a very close-knit family, albeit an occasionally dysfunctional one, and it was a peculiar feeling watching this stranger walk into our midst. It had taken us all quite some time, and a fair amount of pain, to learn to trust each other, meaning juror to juror, juror to bailiff, and bailiff to juror. With all of our problems and issues, we were a family, and this was our household. We knew our habits and our idiosyncrasies. The idea of throwing an unknown entity into this place of unchanging regularity was a bit distressing.

It's not as if we had a choice, and as he walked off the elevator, my first thought was that he looked like a nice enough guy. He was tall with a large build, thick, unkempt gray hair, and a soft face with a wide smile. He said hello and introduced himself to us. Kurt would prove to be as kind and caring as the rest of them, filling in right where Tom left off. I was quite sure he wouldn't hesitate to use one of his weapons, but you couldn't tell by looking at him.

He wore a big wool cap over his head, and Rick and I instantly began calling him "comrade." It was, of course, a term of endearment. Kurt went above and beyond. There was no more use for our juror cards as ice-scrapers—he had the van warmed up and waiting for us in the morning. He went out of his way to make us comfortable. He fit right in.

As Aaron had demonstrated with the television set, they could still work on the trust thing. But nothing detracted from the fact that we were lucky to be in the care of these bailiffs. We were in good hands.

NINETEEN

Day eight of the trial might have been the most horrible day of my entire life. Years later, I still acutely remember how I felt—awash in waves of such sadness that I was entirely unable to escape their embrace.

We first heard from a man who worked at the Red Cross and volunteered with the local 4-H doing highway cleanup. He described a day in October, three months after Beth's disappearance, during which he was collecting litter and had made a crucial discovery.

Deep in the grass, barely perceptible, just beside a small stream, about fifteen feet from the road, lay a purse. Maybe someone had dropped it, or it had somehow fallen out of a vehicle. The witness did what every normal person would do and opened the purse to look for identification.

When asked how he felt when the library card signed by Elizabeth Kutz fell into his hand, he looked down toward the floor, tightened his features, and said he was "really shaken up." I watched as the color drained from his face. In that instant, I felt his pain—the horror, terror, disgust, and repulsion that must have overcome him. It was three months after his gruesome discovery, and I could still see those emotions bound to him like raindrops to a cloud.

I tried to imagine what it must have felt like. I tried to imagine how *I* would have felt, but I couldn't do it. I couldn't separate myself from who I am and what I already knew, and was again struck by how significant and personal a role I was playing in this whole affair.

As terrible as it been to listen to Ellen and the children, this was somehow worse. In a long litany of bad, this was the worst. But not for long.

Another police officer walked up to take the oath. I slid back in my chair to prepare for another "record testimony," as I liked to call it. This was testimony that was primarily for the record, to ensure that the prosecution had all its ducks in a row for appeal or whatever other necessities the legal system hurled at attorneys. "Record testimony" was resoundingly boring and came from law enforcement officers too numerous to count. It often seemed like more empty space, dead air. Once I'd learned to anticipate and identify it, I quickly learned how to put myself in a place where I could pay attention, off-handedly and peripherally, without concentrating so intensely that it exhausted me.

It didn't take long for me to snap back to full attention and realize that I couldn't have been more wrong about this witness. He was a 911 dispatch officer, and he testified about the phone calls he received from and made to Beth Kutz a week before her disappearance. We knew that Beth had taken the kids and moved to her mother's house. We knew that her relationship with Dan had gotten to the point where she felt this was necessary. We knew that Beth was extremely frightened, both for the children and herself. We knew she was confused. We already *knew*. So what was the point of hearing more testimony?

It happened quickly, and I barely had time to prepare myself. For the first time, we jurors were handed something: a transcript of the 911 phone conversations. A deadly silence descended upon the entire courtroom, and the play button was pushed.

I wasn't ready for this. I needed another minute, another eternity to prepare. I knew this woman so well, her family, her likes and dislikes, her fears. All that remained for me was the fact that I'd only seen her face for a couple short seconds and had never heard her voice. She was still a phantom, an apparition. She was still just an image, an entity of my own creation. For days now, I'd been subconsciously pretending she wasn't real.

The eternity ended in three seconds. Beth Kutz was speaking. Beth Kutz was real.

She didn't sound the way I expected, but then how was I to know? Her voice was timid, soft, and I could hear her fear weighing down on her like a never-ending nightmare. Her voice was demure but firm. I could hear her uncertainty about the future, but through it, loud and clear, I heard her resolve. She didn't know what was around the next curve, but she was definitely taking this path. Her mind was made up, and she was leaving her husband. That much was clear.

Despite all of the efforts by the defense to convince us that Beth was still uncertain of what she wanted, that voice told me all I needed. It seemed very clear to me that Beth was scared because she knew Dan was nothing but trouble. Instantly, I was awe-struck by the critical concession I seemed to have just made. Was I really ready to believe this? We had so many fragments, so many puzzle pieces, but this was a turning point.

I could only marginally focus on the conversation and the words lying lifeless in my lap. Too many things were happening at once. Beth Kutz, missing and presumed dead for six months, was in the courtroom talking to us. It was hard for me to focus on *what* was being said more than *who* was saying it. This was not some character that the prosecution had created to befuddle or bewilder us. I could only vaguely remember what Beth looked like, but the defense couldn't—as much as they would have liked to—prevent us from hearing her voice. I am quite sure that they had tried.

Beth was an illusion no more. Her voice, loud and clear, had shattered that. Until this point, it had been easy to live with the phantom. Now we were faced with the reality of a mother, daughter, wife, and sister who was terrified. The reality of a woman that we all now knew so well asking for a police escort to leave her husband on July 20th, one week to the day before she disappeared forever.

I looked around the courtroom, trying to hold back tears. I looked at Beth's family; the hatred toward Dan was gone. Hatred is such a difficult emotion to maintain—it takes strength, vigor, attention, and dedication. Eventually we tire. Eventually, we lose the strength to maintain the fight. Maybe the strength of the hatred can no longer bear the weight of the sadness. Eventually, the hatred has no other choice but to dissipate.

There is, of course, *always* something there to replace it and in this case, it was the most intense, uncontrollable, suffocating, infinite, and profound sadness I have ever seen. I was swallowed in it. I tried to listen dispassionately to the words I knew were being played on some distant tape recorder. I tried to pull myself out to read the word-for-word transcription that lay in my lap somewhere far away, but I just couldn't do it. I was caught in the vortex; there was no escape.

I had been hoping that Beth would walk into the courtroom and had gotten my wish.

Where hatred had been was now hurt. This time there was no hiding the tears on Greg's and David's faces. The veneer was gone. Vern held Ellen and they wept. The poker faces were gone and their grief was on open display for everyone to experience. There was no concern for what anyone thought. Beth's voice filled the courtroom and her family missed her.

I was so powerless; I felt like I was watching some horrific event unfold that I'd known was going to happen but had done nothing about. I was frozen, unable to prevent its occurrence. I tried to move, to help, to prevent everything that was unfolding before us. I couldn't do a thing. I could only watch blindly and stupidly in horror as Beth's family cried what was perhaps their final goodbye.

I suddenly and finally realized with absolute and crushing certainty that it didn't matter how much we all wanted it. It was not going to happen. Beth Kutz was not coming back home.

We now had enough testimony to draw a picture of July 27, 2000. I remembered back to days long past, a number of days that could be counted on two hands, when there was nothing but chaos. It felt like years.

The pieces of the puzzle no longer lay in random discord—they had been put together. It had taken a myriad of seemingly disconnected witnesses, hundreds of unrelated questions, and a lot of time. Taken as a whole, though, there were relationships. In what had seemed like an evolutionary pace, a pattern finally emerged. The puzzle was now nearly complete, and all that remained were the last few pieces that would bring the picture into focus.

TWENTY

By day nine, the isolation was beyond intense. We could scarcely remember a time when we could think and act with anything remotely resembling free will.

We had become like a panel of mannequins in the courtroom—unspeaking, inanimate, immobile.

We were an exhibit. It was cute at first, but no more. We were on display in our own city, among our own friends, coworkers, family members, and acquaintances. We drove past my work every day, and it became less and less familiar. It started out as my workplace, and then it became some place I used to work. By day nine, it was merely a building I could recall with some familiarity, as if I'd once had a friend who'd worked there.

By now, jury selection had already become dreamlike, as if it had happened to someone else. As time goes for the rest of the world, it was but a mere moment ago—a week and a half. It was a barely perceptible ripple, like a second hand on a clock that wavered in super-slow motion before finally clicking into its next position. But time did not work that way in here—instead, time had somehow simultaneously sped up and ground to a complete halt. Seconds crawled and minutes expanded infinitely. It was like the feeling one gets when he pulls into his garage and suddenly realizes he doesn't remember anything from the drive home. This feeling blanketed us like a long shadow, threatening our ability to maintain sanity and stay grounded emotionally and intellectually, as we knew we must.

We knew we still had a long way to go. If the days were to continue to pass as they had so far, I wondered how we would be after yet another week. I had talked to Jessica and Timmy about this, but it seemed unlikely that we were the only jurors who felt this way. Most of the jurors must have been locked in the same emotion, just as we were all locked in the same experience. There was no doubt that this isolation would get more intense before it began to dissipate. The only questions left were how much more of this we could take and, once it was over, whether we would ever know our old lives again. Then suddenly, things changed again, and the beginning of the end was flashed before our eyes.

It was stipulated by both attorneys that what was about to be said served to replace the testimony of a parade of witnesses, who otherwise would have had to swear in and take the stand. In an effort to shorten this already lengthy trial, both attorneys were in agreement and thus we were graced with a thirty-minute Bob Kaiser monologue.

Kaiser explained that there were airline representatives, taxi drivers, and bus companies who said Beth never bought a ticket or availed herself of their particular mode of transportation. The armed forces were unanimous in agreeing that Beth had never joined. Beth had neither applied for nor been accepted into the witness protection program. Beth had neither applied for nor received a passport. Not a single penny had been deposited into or withdrawn from her social security account. Representatives of domestic violence centers could have testified that Beth had not entered their doors.

At this point, the stipulations served only to reiterate what I already knew, and what I suspected most other jurors already knew as well: something terrible had happened to Beth that day in July. We already knew she hadn't run away.

The list went on and on. I remember thinking how thorough it was, how many possibilities had been tracked which I never would have even considered, and how much time this strategy must have saved. However, things were about to change yet again. In what was becoming a common theme, they were going to again change for the worse.

Bob Kaiser, who had eloquently delivered all of these stipulations and, because there were no actual witnesses, had been unable to confuse even one person for a record thirty minutes, stood up and raised two cardboard-backed maps in his arms. One was a map of Dane County and one a map of Columbia County. Both were speckled with purple dots, lines, blobs, and boxes. There were connected lines, shaded areas, and filled-in sections.

"If called to testify," Bob Kaiser began, "various members of Beth Kutz's family would indicate that these are the places where they, over the past six months, have searched for Beth Kutz. They would also testify that, throughout all of these searches, they have uncovered no signs or evidence of Beth Kutz."

The trial dealt yet another crushing blow. I felt the tears blur my vision almost immediately. I strained to see and process what lay before me. Kaiser was speaking in slow motion, and the purple search areas grew in size, from roadsides to yards to blocks to acres to miles. They grew and expanded so monumentally that I could scarcely process the magnitude. The maps grew larger still and with each expansion in my mind, my heart sank lower and lower as I considered the unbelievable effort that this family had put forth, and the disheartening fact that they had barely scratched the surface. They had done so much, and as those maps grew in my mind, the tiny areas that they had searched seemed to proportionately shrink to relative inconsequence.

I found myself staring into another world, with dozens and dozens of friends and family members sitting around someone's house, probably Ellen and Vern's, gathered closely around the kitchen table, staring at maps and organizing who was going to search where, where to start, and where to look next—hours of plotting and planning, organizing and overseeing.

Dozens of them, walking along roads or through fields, trudging through rivers or streams or bogs or marshes, looking behind trees and beneath tall grasses, day after day after day. For what? What did they hope to find? Beth's body? Hour after hour and day after day of praying for closure but not wanting to know what that meant. Searching for some sign of evidence that your daughter, your sister, your friend is no longer. Looking for a sign that she is decomposing in some forgotten place, uncovered and unshielded, her lifeless body long detached from the spirit and soul that made Beth, Beth. Looking for remains that lay unseeing and unknowing, but somehow yearning for peace, sending signals from somewhere, praying for the purest result: find me and reunite me with my family.

My heart went out to her family. Searching and praying that they wouldn't find her dead, that they would return home after yet another terrible, fruitless day of despair to find Beth waiting, a beer in her hand, a smile on her face, laughing at the big joke, and promising that everything would be okay. Her family was going through the unthinkable, praying for and against closure simultaneously, every single day. There could not be peace in that. Ever.

It took about fifteen seconds for all of this to go through my mind, and I was again awash in such abject sadness that I could barely stand to think. From a distance, I heard the words, "Please rise for the jury," and knew I'd have to get up. I did. I walked to the jury room, entered the bathroom, locked the door, and cried. I cried for Beth. I cried for her family and all her friends. I cried for her children. I cried for myself. It had long since been clear that life would never be the same for Beth's family. I now knew, with no doubt at all, that life would never be the same for me. A missing purse, a tape-recorded voice, and a bunch of purple splotches on a map had seen to that. I was now a permanent member of this circle, and I cried for all of us who were locked inside.

We were lined up and led back into the courtroom. Detective Bill Searls stood up from his permanent place alongside the prosecution to take the stand. He'd sat beside the two prosecutors for the entire trial without saying a word. I did not know that someone could hear the entire trial and then testify, but for the millionth time during this process, I was reminded how little I knew about criminal procedure. I guess I finally had to admit that *helping* Lynne through law school was not really the same as *attending* law school, which I had always maintained (always half-joking, of course). I now knew the difference.

The pattern was emerging, and Detective Searls was kind enough to fill in most of the remaining gaps. Once he concluded, the prosecution had painted an effective picture of a summer day nearly six months ago.

On July 27, 2000, Beth Kutz went to work early in the morning. Dan had been stalking her for a few days and Beth was hoping that by going in early, she could avoid him. Ellen hit the road a little later, bringing the children to Kitsie's. They passed Dan, who didn't wave to them and was obviously looking for Beth.

Dan was spotted several times at Demco later that morning. He was confronted by Greg Stahl, who told him, "Get a life, buddy." A police officer arrived moments later. Greg pointed in the direction that Dan had driven, and the officer followed. Thinking Dan was heading toward Highway 51, the policeman went in that direction, just passing the road that led to Dan's brother's house. He didn't find him.

Meanwhile, Dan drove to his brother John's house and convinced John to lend him the Cougar. Dan drove to John's workplace, where the Cougar was parked, left the family Cavalier, and drove away in his brother's car. This was an hour before Beth got off work to head home.

John had gone looking for Beth and Dan later that night with Kelly and Pete (Dan's sister and brother-in-law) and some of Dan's other friends and relatives. They were hoping to find Dan, as Kelly said, "before something happened." They found neither Dan nor

Beth. They did, however, find John's Cougar parked at the corner of Grinde Road and Highway 51, which was exactly where Beth would have had to stop at a stop sign on her way home from work earlier that day.

Beth, meanwhile, had a good morning at work. She talked to numerous friends and her mother several times. She e-mailed the children at Kitsie's. However, over time, Beth became more and more distraught. Several witnesses testified to her change in behavior about midday. It was as if something had happened—perhaps a visit or a phone call—no one was quite sure.

Beth had spent a good part of the afternoon trying to get one of her brothers to accompany her to Kitsie's to pick up the children. Neither was able to do so. She finally reached her mother and said she was on her way home. Ellen agreed to accompany Beth to Kitsie's. Beth asked Ellen to "come looking for me if I'm not home in thirty minutes."

The vice president of the Kutz's bank saw Beth driving a Jeep Cherokee, with personalized plates reading DIDIS, into the 180-acre property at 3:30 p.m. We'd heard a great deal about this Jeep, which Beth had borrowed from her friend Diane the previous week, needing transportation since leaving her husband. A witness named Curt Faga had testified that he saw the same Jeep, with Dan driving, swerving around Highway J about 4:15 p.m. Another witness, Margaret Snorek, testified that she saw the Jeep driving erratically on Mineral Point Road, back in Madison, at 5:55 p.m.

The Jeep was found two days later on Saturday, July 29th, in the Meriter Hospital parking ramp, a couple of miles from Mineral Point Road. It was completely clean except for one lone fingerprint and two drops of blood. The fingerprint belonged to Dan Kutz. It was on the driver's side door, just below the handle.

The two drops of blood belonged to Beth Kutz. They were found in the back of the Jeep, on the carpet that covered the storage area. From the defense's cross-examination, we'd heard a great deal about Beth and her proclivity for biting her fingernails and the possibility that she was menstruating. She had cleaned the back of the Jeep at least once during the previous week.

At 9:15 the night Beth disappeared, Dan had been recorded by a security camera at a Stop-N-Go about seven miles from Meriter Hospital. At 11 p.m., police responded to a call from a nurse who, on her way to work the night shift at Meriter Hospital, called in a pedestrian walking the wrong way along Highway CV just north of the Stop-N-Go.

Dan Kutz was picked up with no shoes, no shirt, wet pants, and a dazed appearance. He told the officer that he'd been riding with some strangers and left his boots in their car. He couldn't identify the people or the make or color of the car. The police took him to his brother's house. His brother testified that Dan said only one thing upon arriving: "You can have sex with them and they still leave you."

Later that night, after Beth had been reported missing, several detectives took Dan in again. He told a completely different story to these officers. Dan said that he'd gotten in the Jeep with Beth, they had talked for several hours, and had actually reconciled. He said they drove to a park and had sex. They were hungry and went to get food. She dropped him off at the Stop-N-Go after reconciling, and he didn't realize until he was in the store and Beth was gone that he'd left his boots in the Jeep. He never indicated having gone to the 180-acre property.

The following weekend, Dan's key to his brother's Cougar was found at the 180-acre property, along the edge of the driveway. The Cavalier was found at John's workplace. In its trunk, police found a blanket and several boxes containing hundreds of photographs. Dan's pants were checked for DNA, and there was evidence of both his semen and Beth's vaginal fluid on the back of his jeans. Dan's watch was also checked for DNA and tested positive for a drop of Beth's blood.

Early on the morning of July 28th, Dan Kutz was arrested for the disappearance of his wife.

That was the puzzle. It was nearly complete, and it was up to us to fill in the remaining pieces, as best we could, in deliberations. This was a murder trial, and I knew that one of the hardest decisions I would ever have to make still lay before me. Because of that, I felt that there was still a lot missing.

Bob Kaiser stood up and cleared his throat: "The State rests."

I couldn't believe it. For some reason I had assumed that the prosecution was going to take at least a few more weeks. It just hadn't seemed that it would ever end or that there could ever be enough information. I still needed more. I wasn't ready for the defense to poke holes in this—there were enough holes already. I needed more answers. Given that Searls had nearly completed the puzzle for us, I didn't know what was bothering me, what was still missing. I just knew something was. It wouldn't be until deliberations that I would figure out why I was having such a hard time.

I really wasn't ready for this trial to end. Though the isolation was incredibly intense, I had developed a certain comfort in it. We walked into the jury room and stood around with mouths agape for some time before someone said, "Wow, I can't believe the prosecution is finished." It was clear from the look on everyone's faces that the feeling was unanimous.

The prosecution's case had lasted nine and a half days. I tried to imagine how we would feel if the defense were to last as long.

It didn't.

Actually, the defense was not that exciting. In fact, it built on one theme and basically hammered it home with unwavering rigidity. It started with a Meriter nurse and worked its way through a dozen more Meriter nurses, a Capital Police officer (the unit that patrols downtown Madison), several Meriter patients and security guards, and a dozen do-gooders with no connection to the case whatsoever.

Every one of them had only one thing to say: "I saw the Jeep." It was always sometime late Thursday night, Friday, or Saturday morning. Dan would have been in custody during all of these times. The Jeep was finally found at about 1 p.m. on Saturday.

The testimony and sightings, if true, would have completely crumbled the prosecution's entire theory or, at the very least, introduced very reasonable doubt.

"Are you sure you saw the Jeep? Green Jeep Cherokee?"

"Yes."

"What did the license plate read?"

"DIDIS."

"Are you sure those were the plates? How can you be sure?"

A dozen iterations of this one. "I remember thinking, it must be Deedee's car."

Or, "I was wondering what die-die meant."

Or, "My dog is named Deedee, and I thought it would be perfect for her."

And finally, "Are you absolutely positive it read DIDIS? Could it have said DIDIT? Or DEDE?"

"No. I'm sure."

"How did you know this was important? What made you call it in?"

Another dozen variations, but most focused on seeing the Jeep in the news a few days later as it was being towed away from Meriter to the police impound lot for scrutiny. "I saw it on the news, and thought I'd better call it in."

Witnesses had seen the Jeep everywhere, from the northwest side of Madison to the southeast side. Early in the morning, late in the evening. Many were unsure who was driving. Some testified that it was a thin woman with short curly hair and sunglasses. Some testified that it was a male. Others stated that two people were in the Jeep.

The defense kept them coming, one after another. It was unbelievable. I didn't know what to think of this. Could the Jeep really have been seen around Madison? Dan was in custody by then. If it was out and about, who was driving? Was the woman with sunglasses Beth? Did Dan have an accomplice? Was it possible that his story was true, and Beth was abducted later that night? Did Beth just leave the family and run away herself?

The defense managed to raise a number of questions in my mind. The puzzle started fracturing and splitting at the seams.

Scenes that I thought were clear and accurate started fading and blurring. Suddenly, I started feeling like it was the beginning of the trial again. I began wondering, yet again, what we really knew. Neither for the first nor last time, I realized we didn't know very much.

The defense called Dan's priest. A good friend of the Kutz's, he testified about the marital problems the family was facing. But he also gave us a side of Dan we hadn't seen: a Dan who took care of and loved his children and who helped out around the church. I couldn't really tell what the priest thought, but it seemed as though he was generally fond of the defendant.

Another puzzle piece shattered.

Dan's sister took the stand. An editor and photographer for a Native American magazine from northern Wisconsin, we were all drawn to her immediately. She was clearly troubled by this whole thing. It seemed that, while she was a good friend of Beth's, she also was fond of her brother and wanted to support him.

Things were getting increasingly discordant, and I was getting increasingly stressed. I had been praying that I would not be chosen as an alternate—I had wanted to see this through to the end, and I still did. There was a rapidly growing part of me, however, that was beginning to wonder whether I really wanted to have anything more to do with this experience at all.

TWENTY-ONE

It was the third Monday of the trial, and I could tell right away it was going to be a very strange day. I was very tired, and it was really hard to get up. I think we were all physically, mentally, emotionally, and most of all, spiritually exhausted. There is no good way to articulate the effect that this isolation, combined with the horrible testimony, was having on us. Each night I tried to do so in my journal, and each night I reread what I had written and shook my head at how woefully short I had fallen.

We arrived at the courthouse wearied and ill-prepared for another long day. It wasn't the first time we began really late, so we just sat around, discontented and frustrated. The creeping malaise was widespread; neither Rick nor Jessica wanted to hack. I looked around at the despondent funeral service surrounding the jury room and wondered if this is what the room always looked like during break. It was the first time since day two that we'd been in here, instead of "Hackland," for more than a moment. If this was how things had been, I quite simply would have gone mad. It was clear Rick and Jessica agreed, because we soon got up to hack. I ended up being glad we did, because it was another thirty minutes before the magical words came drifting back, "They are ready."

Little happened once we arrived in the courtroom. It was about as boring as sitting in the jury room had been. There were two witnesses, neither of whom said anything especially enlightening, and we were released for yet another break. At this point, there was really no good reason we hadn't been allowed to sleep until 10 a.m., which just pissed us off even more. This break was pretty long as well, after which we finally re-entered the courtroom and were absolutely stunned to hear the words we weren't expecting for at least two more days.

"Your Honor, the defense rests."

The end was rapidly approaching, which simultaneously shocked, excited, and scared the hell out of me. The prosecution performed their rebuttal, after which we had another break, were brought back in to watch the attorneys approach the bench for ten minutes, and finally heard the trial's final words:

"State rests."

My first thought was, "That's it? No more testimony? I have to make a decision based on this? It's not enough!"

My second thought was even more profound and confusing. "What is happening here?" I had missed my life so much—being home with Lynne and our dogs, going wherever I wanted whenever I wanted, and the anonymity of it all. I missed my life. So why was I feeling depressed about this ordeal being almost over? After sixteen days, how could there remain some unknown place, deep inside of me, that had grown attached to this and didn't want it to end?

I'd miss my new friends. There is a special quality to new friendships—its brilliance flashes infrequently and only for a short time before it fades to normalcy. There was something rare between Rick, Jessica, and me. There was something about the isolation and stress and shared experience of this existence that had accelerated, deepened, and somehow intensified this bond.

I knew I would miss being taken care of, having no worries or responsibilities. I didn't have to do laundry, shop for groceries, or cook. I didn't have to work, pay bills, or worry about the mortgage. I didn't have to think or plan or multitask. It was all done for me and, sadly, I knew I would miss it.

Beneath all these feelings, I knew there was one solitary reason that I was so reluctant and frightened to reach the end. I was about to face the most difficult decision of my life, and I wasn't ready to make it.

Ready or not, the time had come.

Stephen King, in his book "Rita Hayworth and the Shawshank Redemption," called it "institutionalized." The process by which a prisoner comes to depend on his prison, an abductee begins to relate to her kidnapper. It's hard to believe, but I have to admit it had happened to me. I'd been flirting with this feeling for awhile, but the proximity of conclusion exploded it to the surface.

I've experienced culture shock before upon returning home after travels abroad, but what I was facing now was clearly going to be a different kind. All of a sudden I would have to take control of my own life again, make decisions, and consider repercussions and consequences. It just kept hitting me again and again, reminding me how rote and repetitive my life had been here. I was scared and amazed to find myself admitting a certain comfort with this world.

For four of us, the end was near. After all of this, four names, chosen randomly from a hat, would determine who would be sent home and prevented from participating in deliberations. Robbed of the closure we *all* deserved. To have that happen would make everything seem worthless. Of course, that would not be true; we had each played a role in this crucial process of the judicial system, and we had each helped to shape some of this experience for the rest of us. Even if some of us did not take part in the voting process, we would have still contributed to the verdict.

Nonetheless, I did not want to be chosen as an alternate. It would feel like climbing Mount Everest and getting airlifted off only a few meters from the summit. I was greedy, and I didn't want Rick or Jessica to be chosen as alternates. They were my court companions, and I needed to share the whole thing with them. But I knew they wouldn't be chosen as alternates. Jessica *knew* she would be here for deliberations. We had talked about it, and I admired her absolute confidence. I am such a chicken in these matters—I would never be brazen enough to vocalize my contention that something I wanted would come true. For me, things don't work that way.

Still, it was not Jessica I was worried about—it was me. Jessica had such good ideas for how to organize and facilitate deliberations, how to get along and reach consensus, and how to ensure that every voice was heard. We had spent many nights discussing what this would be like. I couldn't think of a single person here who would have added as much value to this process as she would. That's why I knew she would be there.

So I kept on quietly worrying about myself. I wished I could stop thinking, stop focusing on how badly I wanted to see this thing through. Part of it was institutionalization, yes. But it was much more than that. It was an absolute, profound need for closure. I thought about it constantly, which only served to make my imminent dismissal that much more distressing.

Way back in jury selection, I remember thinking, "I'll be honest and let the chips fall where they may. If I'm chosen, great. If not, great. I can live with the results, whatever they may be." I wished I could find that level of serenity right now—a way to remember that these impending realities represent a burden I could live without carrying. But for some reason, I couldn't do it. Either way, I knew that in all likelihood we would find out the next day, Tuesday, and the waiting would be over.

I thought about Lynne, my own bed, and my dogs. I thought about going home to them. It didn't sound bad. I thought about this being my last night here. I shuddered, turned out the light, closed my journal, and then my eyes. I missed my wife. I didn't know what I wanted. I lay awake for a long time and tried to prepare myself for the devastation I knew was coming.

Twenty-Two

The wake-up knock on Tuesday seemed almost surreal—I knew it could be the last one. We had breakfast and hit the road. There was mostly silence; we were all locked in the solitary confinement of our thoughts.

Jessica, Rick, and I hacked for a while. We were all nervous; we knew that alternates were going to be selected in the near future, probably right after closing arguments. We knew at some point that we would get another break, possibly our last, before four of our co-jurors and friends were summarily dismissed.

We walked into the courtroom prepared to hear closings, and the judge said he was going to choose the alternates right then. This didn't make sense: how was it possible, after all this time and all this testimony, that four people wouldn't even be there for closing arguments? It didn't seem fair and, honestly, it seemed kind of stupid. What if someone got sick during deliberations? Shouldn't the alternate have heard the closings?

The moment I had dreaded was here. I prayed that I wouldn't be an alternate. The judge drew names from a hat.

So many things went through my head during those moments. I needed closure. I needed to be there until the end. I was shaking and resigning myself to the inevitable.

Blake was selected. I wasn't sure he wanted to be here anyway, so I was happy for him. Although I liked him, he and I weren't really close, so this was okay with me. One down, three to go.

Timmy was chosen next. This was a bummer. He was my friend, and I would miss having him around, but I was happy for him because he wanted out and missed his family. His isolation seemed worse than ours, and the Timmy who had wanted to be on this jury was long gone.

Stacy was next. I had immensely enjoyed Stacy's insights and sense of humor and was very sad to see her go. I also knew she had wanted to be here until the end, maybe as much as I did.

Stacy and Timmy. I was glad it wasn't me, but these were two of my four closest friends. That didn't seem right. My friends from day one, way back as untouchables in jury selection, were now standing up and walking away. This may very well be the last time that I would ever see them. This was harder than I thought, and I thought I had been prepared for the worst.

It was suddenly very empty, as jurors #14 and #16 walked away, leaving an empty seat to my immediate left and my immediate right. I was sure that I wouldn't be alone for long, because the last one was going to be me. There was no doubt about it.

It wasn't. It was Jessica. I was shell-shocked. I hadn't even thought of that. My excitement at not being chosen was completely dwarfed by the sting. Of my four closest friends on the jury, those I respected most, three were chosen. My closest friend was chosen. It had crossed my mind that she'd be deliberating without me; it had never crossed my mind that I'd be deliberating without her.

I had to force myself to breathe. Five minutes earlier, we had been hacking. Now, without any kind of goodbye or good luck, Jessica was walking away and going home. I turned and looked as she walked by my seat in slow motion. She gave me a small smile as she walked by that said that it was okay, despite what must have been crushing disappointment. I knew that it wasn't okay—for her or for me.

Sixteen of us had come into this together and merged to a single entity. After fifteen straight days and nights with the same people, routine, and experiences, a full fourth of our group was now gone. Immediately, the box seemed extraordinarily empty and ten times bigger.

For Jessica and Stacy, who had wanted to stay, I can't imagine the pain and hurt they must have felt at being splintered from this experience, both from the group itself and from the closure that we all needed. This process was terrible, and I was angry. It seemed inexcusable to have sixteen of us go through this experience for so long and then not allow us to see it through together until the very end. It was so lonely and empty for those of us who remained. Just four people were gone, but it had the emotional impact of four hundred. Things felt quiet, different. I felt a supreme sense of loss, partially over losing my friends, but also over the fragmentation of our group.

Each juror brought something unique and powerful to this trial. There was no doubt in my mind that during deliberations, we were going to need every iota of that uniqueness, power, personality, and individuality at the table. With one-fourth of those strengths now missing, we would have to re-create our group dynamic in order to function without them. In less than an instant, Jessica, Timmy, Stacy, and Blake were through the door and gone. I could barely focus on what happened in the next hour.

Lyn Opelt stood up to close for the prosecution. Over the past several weeks, we had grown to know and respect this woman as a fine attorney, but she was nowhere near as dramatic or entertaining as Kaiser or Burke. We'd never even considered the possibility that she would close; we would have all bet the ranch it would be Bob Kaiser.

Ms. Opelt stood and spoke for two and a half hours about why Beth wouldn't leave, why Beth didn't leave, why Dan had to have murdered her. She ran back over hours and hours of testimony, summarizing and reorganizing. The closing did little for me; it didn't sway me significantly one way or the other.

The biggest jolt came about an hour into Opelt's closing, when Jessica and Stacy walked back into the courtroom as observers and sat in the back of the room. I was thrilled, because I'd known that both wanted to be there until the end, and I was saddened by how depressed they must have been to be missing this. I was glad they made it back in time to see the majority of Opelt's closing; they really hadn't missed very much.

When she finished, I reminded myself how many holes still existed: in spite of all the puzzle pieces that the prosecution had magically woven together to form an entirely plausible scenario, Dan Kutz was still innocent until proven guilty. And while a picture was nice, pictures could be doctored. I was still unconvinced as to its authenticity.

The jurors had developed such an array of impressions of Dan's attorney, Dennis Burke, over the past three weeks. We had nodded in agreement and shaken our heads in disgust. There were so many times we had laughed at his mannerisms, his sense of humor, and his shocking rudeness. More than anything, however, we were impressed with his intellect, showmanship and skills as an attorney.

Dennis Burke stepped before us and looked into our eyes before he even said a word. I knew then that this was going to be powerful. He had notes, but he would refer to them only occasionally.

He started by speaking of the first murder trial in Wisconsin history, way back in 1847. He spoke of what a terrible tragedy that case was and how, in that regard, it was similar to this one. He offered condolences to Beth's family and explained that he never intended to slight them or cast doubt upon them in any way, and if he had implied that, then let him apologize right now. The fact remained that he needed to make it look as though Beth had disappeared of her own accord, and thus had no choice but to cast shadows upon her character.

He looked troubled, concerned, and compassionate. It was the same look he had displayed in jury selection all those years ago, when the general consensus was that we liked this man. It was the look that was almost enough to convince us of his sincere, profound belief that there were too many questions and too much doubt to vote guilty. If he believed that, why shouldn't we believe him?

Burke began raising questions. He raised just a suggestion of doubt, tantalizing us with it, and then began to manipulate, reshape, and expand it. He reminded us of the Jeep sightings, asking, "How can you firmly believe the prosecution's two key Jeep sighting witnesses, Snorek and Faga, but not believe our twenty or so witnesses?"

How could we? What had made their two witnesses more credible? It was a good question, and like a million others, I didn't know the answer.

Then something unbelievable happened. Burke admitted that Beth was dead and not just missing. I couldn't breathe, or even blink. Every cell of my being was focused on what this man was saying and the way in which he was saying it. This was a *huge* admission and definitely the first time we'd heard him say anything like it. He'd spent a large part of his cross-examinations going after the possibility that Beth had disappeared, bringing up cashed checks and unaccounted-for dollars, continually reminding us of her two stints with infidelity and her late arrivals at home after secret rendezvous with Greg Stahl.

Burke then admitted that Dan and Beth had gone to the 180-acre property. "The key to the Cougar was found there; of course they went there," he said, "we don't dispute that." This was absolutely the first admission by any member of the defense that this had happened. When he said this, I started to have a sinking feeling, as though their strategy was a ball of yarn, and it had somehow escaped their possession and was now unraveling before our eyes. It was confusing and troubling to watch.

Regarding the numerous Jeep sightings, Burke said, "These are good people, God bless them, who have come forward from their jobs and their lives to help us solve this case, help us in our search for truth. There were so many. And I'm so scared that I'm going to overwhelm you with all these sightings, but it just goes to demonstrate how much doubt there is here."

It was true. There was doubt. They couldn't all have been wrong, could they?

"There are so many things I want to say to you guys," he kept saying. My heart went out to him. He was so believable and convincing. I was absolutely riveted to him—his mannerisms, his words, his actions.

He referred to our courage and commended us for it. He ridiculed the prosecution and their witnesses, but he did it in a kind way. "I'm not out to embarrass them," he said. Or, "It was not meant to make them look bad." "These are good people, and if you ever inferred differently, I stand corrected." He spoke of loss. He pulled at us, playing on our strong reluctance and disgust at orphaning two young children. He tugged hard, and it hurt.

Other than the admissions, Dennis Burke gave the best closing I could have imagined. Maybe in some way the admissions even helped, because we already believed them anyway. Movie and television directors should have been in the audience. After a lifetime of watching courtroom dramas, I had high expectations for this trial that were never met. A real trial is not like a TV trial. Real trials are long and tedious and full of "legalese." They are full—literally *full*—of dead air. I'd reached the point where I was sure the closing would be the same way: boring and monotone. Opelt's closing validated my belief, as she went through the evidence and reminded us of all the facts we needed to keep in mind during deliberations. It wouldn't have kept a TV audience tuned in. Burke, however, was right out of a movie. He was passionate, emotional, and dramatic. More important, he was convincing. He finished and thanked us for serving. He wished God's blessing upon us.

He sat down and I knew. Right then, I knew. I was one-hundred percent positive. There was no reasonable doubt. There was no doubt at all.

There was absolutely no way I was going to find Dan Kutz guilty of first-degree intentional homicide.

Bob Kaiser was a character, that's for sure. He was emotional, passionate, ornery, quick-tempered, and humorous. He could just as easily fly off the handle and yell at his own witness as he could crack a huge, goofy smile.

I remember thinking during jury selection that he was rude and inconsiderate of jurors in the box. I didn't think he'd acted in a way that demonstrated he had any, much less full, appreciation of what the potential jurors were about to sacrifice. Jury selection was where Bob Kaiser made his first impression on me; he'd made a lot of impressions since.

Bob Kaiser had an innate and uncanny ability to render any and all witnesses entirely confused and fully flustered. Of the seventy-six witnesses the state had called, I would estimate that he confused at least eighty percent of them on at least one occasion. In spite of everything, though, he had impressed us immensely.

Humorous, intelligent, and confusing, the man of the crazy hair flip and constant eyeglass push, Bob Kaiser stepped to the plate to rebut. None of us knew what to expect, and there was no way we could have predicted what was about to come. He started by glaring at us. He shook his head back and forth. He started quietly, but took off like a missile launch.

He flung his hands and arms wildly in the air. His eyes bore down upon us like a hawk nearing its prey. He paced back and forth, to the lectern and to the jury, to the exhibits and to the witness stand. He marched right in front of us, literally inches, with trembling lips and fiery eyes. His face grew animated, turned red, boiled with anger, then calmed, and reverted again.

He grabbed exhibits and photographs and shoved them in our faces, reminding us how clear and convincing the stories were. He varied tones constantly, alternating between hushed whispers and resounding screeches. He was a man possessed. It was too much, and I was truly shocked at what I was seeing. Because of this, one could not help but focus on his dramatics, and it took serious self-control to not break out laughing. "Okay, Bob, good acting," I wanted to say. "Now let's get back to the case." Right then, Kaiser pulled out the maps and pointed decidedly at their meaning and clarity. I remembered them well and was instantly sobered back to reality.

It readily became clear that while *how* he was speaking was amusing, *what* he was saying was most certainly not. Evidence and testimony and theories flew from his mouth. It was overwhelming. There were the comments Dan had made in the past about "burying us" and "never seeing the children again." There was Dan's anger over Greg Stahl, and how he wanted to save the land. There were the pictures in the trunk of the Cavalier, and the escalation of violent behavior. The day of Beth's disappearance, Dan had switched cars with his brother. He had forced himself into Beth's car, and forced her to have sex with him. He had not let her call her family. There was the key at the 180-acre property, the blood in the Jeep and on his watch, and the sole fingerprint on the Jeep. There were Dan's lies to his brother and the police that night.

Throughout his entire closing and all the strong, valid, convincing, passionate, and wholly reasonable points he made, one stood out like a single star in a pitch black sky:

"Who else?"

This was something new. Never mind that it had not been introduced earlier in the trial; I couldn't fathom how I'd never considered it. Who else would find and abduct Beth on that particular night, after she and Dan had parted ways? Who else would kill Beth on July 27th, the night the redemption period ended?

The question rose and hung over us like a storm cloud: Who else would have any reason to hide Beth's body? Who else would dream that her family would search this hard for her? Who else would need to separate himself, as a stranger, from the crime so profoundly? The questions almost held the weight of the case on their own. In a reaction with which I was growing increasingly accustomed, I had no answers.

With a shake of his head, a flip of his hair, and a deep breath, Bob Kaiser finished. I was going to be sick. While leaving the courtroom, I managed one quick glance to Stacy and Jessica, who seemed very small and distant in the back of the courtroom. I hope they understood what was behind that glance, because I have never felt anything so profoundly with all of my being: "I wish you guys were here right now, but I hope you realize how lucky you are that you aren't."

We were as quiet as sleep in the jury room. Cold pizza was waiting for us, and we ate silently and somberly. Had I really been praying that I wouldn't be selected as an alternate? What the hell was I thinking? I couldn't even begin to focus or consider what we were about to face. For one of the few times in my life, I was utterly dumbstruck. Looking around, it was clear I was not alone. The end of trial, the selection of alternates, and two incredibly powerful closings, all in a very short period of time, had left us completely bewildered.

If I'd had the time or inclination to stop and think about what was really happening, to reconnect with reality, I'm sure I would have lost it. Reality was all around us, and it was entirely too unbearable to try on for size, much less bring home.

The judge called us back to the courtroom for jury instructions. We lined up and I was at the end, with no Stacy in front of me and no Timmy behind me. We'd done this a thousand times in the exact same way, and all of a sudden it was completely different.

I had had high hopes for jury instructions, and sadly they failed to meet even my lowest expectations. We would discuss this later in deliberations, and I would get nearly unanimous concurrence among the other jurors. The judge read what we were to do, how we were to reach reasonable doubt, by "searching for the truth, not for doubt," and what each of the charges were and how they were legally defined. There was a lot of repetition from day one, but also some new stuff.

We were tired. The judge's words were like a light breeze. I heard them and knew they were there, but they were more like background noise. I was unable to digest or internalize most of what he said. I knew we would receive copies of the instructions in the deliberation room; I also knew we would have to reread each of them more than once.

The judge had given us no instructions on how we were to deliberate, no recommendations for a process, no thoughts for choosing a foreman or getting started. For all the questions we had, we received nothing. At this point, it didn't matter much to me.

We walked slowly and quietly with bowed heads back to the vans. The feeling of despondency and dejection did not lessen as we rode back to the hotel and then headed toward our rooms. I walked down the hall and passed by Jessica's empty room. I walked into my bathroom and threw up until my sides ached and tears ran down my face. After expunging anything of substance that remained in my system, I sat down next to the toilet and cried yet again. I didn't want to imagine what tomorrow was going to be like, and I was lucky to have enough tears to thoroughly blur my vision.

I walked down to Rick's room to chat. He was tired and getting ready for bed. We talked for a few minutes, but I could tell he wanted to sleep, and I guess I did, too. I wanted to talk to him about Jessica being chosen as an alternate, but it seemed too strange. We said good night and I went back to my room. I lay in bed, staring at the shadows that danced across my ceiling. I spent most of the night trying unsuccessfully to discern their meaning. I was still staring at the ceiling when a knock came at the door, telling me the end was about to begin.

There was no more judge, evidence, attorneys, or witnesses. There were no more tears, stories, pictures, or horror. There were only twelve sad, troubled people, and the weight of a million worlds hanging heavily upon us. There was nothing left except us—our bents and biases, our impressions and ideals.

Deliberation time had arrived.

PART THREE:

In Judgment

(Deliberations)

Twenty-Three

I wanted to be foreman. I'd acted like a joker for most of the three weeks of trial and knew that many people retained that impression of me. There was the unfortunate incident regarding rubber bands, and that terrible tragedy of the paper football in the restaurant. But I was nonetheless ready to lobby for the job. I knew everyone, respected everyone, and trusted my ability to facilitate meetings and organize thinking in a way that ensured we would move forward in a positive direction. I knew I could help lead the way to consensus.

Things were so serious here, so intense. We needed someone who could help keep things on an even keel, who could study each person carefully and make sure he or she was okay with what we were discussing, why we were discussing it, and where we were headed. One who could ensure that everyone had an opportunity to offer input and to be heard.

I knew that I would be good at the job; it was so critical that we did this right. I was extremely anxious about entering such an undefined nebula, despite the fact that these thoughts had been going through my mind, at some level, since the minute I had walked into jury selection all those moons ago.

Deliberations represented a complete and utter shift in the direction we had been headed for the previous fourteen days. And, in an act of imperceptible coincidence, it occurred in a room that might allow us to embark upon this new journey in an unbiased, concentrated way. We were to deliberate in Jury Room 2, the only room in our entire existence with which we were not intimately familiar.

There was a gigantic oval table taking up the majority of the room. Around it sat twelve uncomfortable plastic chairs. There was a small rolling blackboard in the far corner to the left. To our right were the typical and unglamorous men's and women's rooms that we had used with regularity. Dull white walls, a plasterboard ceiling, and a stained, linoleum-like floor surrounded us. It was hard to imagine twelve people crowded into this room.

To our immediate left, lining the entire wall and then some, were boxes upon maps upon envelopes upon bags of every exhibit that we had been privileged to receive into evidence over the past two-plus weeks. There was so much, it was unbelievable. Had there really been that many exhibits presented? One small picture here, one insignificant boot there. They had seemed so random and inconsequential back then. Here, in this already small room, they stacked high, wide, and mighty.

The room couldn't have been more than fifteen by twenty-five feet, 375 square feet at the most. The table and chairs took up about a third of the room. Along the three-and-a-half-foot divide between the table and one of the walls, running lengthwise across the room from front door to back wall, were the exhibits. To the right of that, along the back wall, was the blackboard. Directly across from the evidence, on the right side of the table, there'd be enough room to walk by if everyone sitting along the table scooted in. There was a good space directly in front of us, between the close end of the table and the bathroom doors, probably ten by five feet or so. It wasn't huge, but it was at least space for us to stand and stretch.

The room felt smaller than my bedroom closet. We ambled in, slowly measuring what was about to become our new home. Lori reminded us, "This door will be closed and locked at all times. If you ever need anything, you can knock and either Kurt or I will help you and try to get you what you need."

She wished us luck and closed the door. I wished I was home, and took a seat.

As soon as we walked into the room and the door was closed behind us, foreman selection was over. At least three jurors instantly appointed James our foreman. They sat him down at the head of the table, simultaneously exclaiming, "James is our foreman." Before anyone could say a thing, he agreed. James was a second-year law student, and obviously that was the criterion that was most important to some of the jurors. I was pretty disappointed, both because of the lack of an intelligent process and my desire to be foreman, but I quickly decided it wasn't worth fighting over. I did believe that the foreman should be fair, balanced, and, above all else, a good facilitator—I was ready to jump in to ensure those things, if necessary.

Jodi and I both started by saying that we should set some ground rules. The twelve of us agreed on a few, namely that we respect each other, listen, not get personal, not interrupt, and most importantly, agree to not leave the room until we were all comfortable. Those words would come back to haunt me, and probably will for the rest of my life.

We decided to start with the less serious charges and work our way forward. I thought this was a good idea because it would set the stage for the harder stuff and give us a positive base on which we could hopefully build. The defendant was charged with four counts: first-degree intentional homicide, stalking, obstruction of justice, and hiding a corpse.

I had once believed that I understood the magnitude of what we were facing. We had spent so much time planning and preparing for it. Maybe we had been purposefully fooling ourselves all along. Maybe it was an unconscious separation from reality, initiated by an internal survival mechanism over which we have no control. Nonetheless, it wasn't enough. It wasn't until we looked down at those four charges that we really understood the enormity of what stared back at us.

Stalking and obstruction of justice sounded unpleasant. First-degree murder and hiding a corpse sounded *appalling*. This was not going to be easy.

We started with the stalking charge, which seemed to be straightforward. Beth was obviously frightened of Dan and wanted to get away from him. Dan obviously wanted Beth back and was not going to leave her alone until he had what he wanted. Beth even went to the courthouse to obtain a restraining order.

Of course, like everything else in this experience, the stalking charge would prove to be nowhere near as straightforward as we'd imagined. To find a defendant guilty of stalking, the jury must find beyond a reasonable doubt that the defendant "intentionally engaged in a course of conduct directed at a specific person that caused that person to fear and that would cause a reasonable person to fear bodily injury or death and where the actor knew or reasonably should have known that the conduct placed the person in reasonable fear of bodily injury or death."

It was so confusing and perplexing that we had to read it five times. According to the count, we had to look into three separate elements:

A. *Dan intentionally engaged in a course of conduct directed at Beth inducing fear of bodily injury or death.*

   "Intentionally engaged" meant that Dan acted with purpose.

   "Course of conduct" meant that Dan maintained a visual or physical proximity to Beth on two or more calendar days in Dane County, Wisconsin.

B. *A reasonable person would fear bodily injury or death in that position.*

"Reasonable person" was defined as someone of ordinary intelligence or prudence.

C. *The defendant knew or should have known that the course of conduct in which he was engaging placed Beth in reasonable fear of death or bodily injury.*

Element A was difficult because Dan and Beth lived in Columbia County, Wisconsin, not Dane. Beth's parents house was in Columbia, as were both pieces of land that Dan and Beth owned.

Element B was difficult because, in twelve years of marriage, Dan had never lifted a finger against Beth. It's hard to demonstrate fear of bodily injury from a person who has never caused bodily injury in the past. Element B also asked us, despite this fact, to find that Beth both was a reasonable person and did indeed maintain this fear.

Element C was difficult because it forced us to assess not only Beth's state of mind but also Dan's ability to read it. All of a sudden, what had seemed to be an easy charge to discuss looked inconceivably complex and difficult. It did, however, still look better than murder.

The final Sunday of the trial, two days before the alternates were selected and dismissed, Jessica, Timmy, and I were talking at the end of the hall where I always sat and played my guitar. Timmy mentioned how frustrating it would be if, during deliberations, other jurors wanted to re-create the entire trial. He felt we should have our decisions made by then—after two weeks of testimony, he thought it should be pretty clear to all of us. "We all heard the same thing, we all should feel the same way," Timmy had said.

Jessica and I had vehemently disagreed. We both said that the likelihood of that happening was slim, and a much more feasible scenario included a great deal of dissention and disagreement. We felt there was a reason twelve people were sent into a room. We felt there was a reason that the process was called "deliberations."

People can hear things differently. One juror might see a witness as nervous and thus call her credibility into question. Another might believe that very same witness to be the most important of the entire case. Deliberations would be our chance to go over things, re-create and re-evaluate, and tie loose pieces together in ways that witnesses or attorneys may have been unable. Jessica and I were both very anxious to be in that final twelve. This give and take, this opportunity to share information and ideas, and this chance to work together as a group and zero in on a target, were some of biggest reasons why.

Jessica was long gone by now, but she would have been proud of our process. Timmy was also long gone, and he would have been disgusted by it. We began poring over the evidence, re-assessing our notes and our memories. It was exactly as I had hoped—dynamic, engaging, and productive. The testimony, evidence, and witnesses from the previous fourteen days flooded back into our existence as we scrutinized our notes and memories.

We were perturbed with the fact that we were only allowed to search in Dane County and not use any of the examples that occurred in Columbia County. We sent our first question to the judge about 11 a.m.:

> *"In considering the stalking charge, is the jury only to consider acts and evidence occurring within the borders of Dane County and not Columbia County?"*

It seemed likely that it would be awhile before we received a response, so we continued working. Finally, a knock came at the door and our answer arrived.

> *"As long as any portion of the conduct occurred within Dane County, you may consider these activities to the extent that they fit within the instruction of stalking."*

We were disappointed and frustrated by an answer that we didn't find to be especially enlightening; however, we decided it meant what we had feared—that we had to look at Dane County only. I didn't understand why this hurdle had been created before us. Everyone knew that most of Dan and Beth's days were spent in Columbia County. How on earth was it even *possible* that they not be included?

Luckily, once we began searching, it didn't take us long to find three days in Dane County. On July 22nd, in DeForest, while Beth was shopping, Dan pulled up in front of her car and slammed on his brakes, forcing her to stop. They got into an intense argument and were yelling in front of the children. At least one witness remembered seeing Dan at Demco (Beth's place of employment, also in Dane County) on July 25th or 26th. And Dan had been seen at Demco on that fateful day, July 27th. We had three days, so Element A (visual proximity) was satisfied.

Element B was a little more difficult. We tried to assess Beth's fear on those particular dates. How could we do that? We didn't know what she felt on those days or any days for that matter. We didn't know what effect Dan's behavior had on Beth's state of mind on *those* particular days. How could we? How could anyone? It was very frustrating, and we were getting nowhere, going back and forth about what may or may not have happened and what Beth may or may not have felt.

We finally laid to rest that line of thinking and began pursuing a different angle. We decided that although time and place were necessary for Element A, they were not relevant for Element B, which dealt with Beth's state of mind. Fear can be based on an intensification and accumulation of prior experience. We decided that, if on those three days, Beth felt fear of bodily injury, this element would be satisfied, even if that fear was based on prior events that had led to her state of mind on those particular days.

The previous couple of months had demonstrated a vast increase in Dan's aggressive and violent behavior. We'd heard testimony about comments he had made such as, "If you leave me, they'll bury all four of us on the hill" and "If you leave me, you'll never see your children again." Dan had locked Beth in the bathroom and she'd bruised her arm climbing out. He'd made the children cry on more than one occasion.

When Beth finally moved out, she'd called 911 to request a "keep the peace" officer to accompany her back to the house and make sure everything went okay while she got her things. We remembered the 911 tape played during the trial and how we could hear the fear in her voice as she asked for help.

It was hard to keep track of all the examples. Of course, one indication of Beth's fear was so prominent that it nearly rendered all others meaningless. On July 27th, the day she disappeared, she called her mother just before leaving work. Knowing that Dan had been following her around that day, she said, "If I'm not home in thirty minutes, come looking for me."

We had satisfied most of Element B; all that remained was our belief that Beth was a reasonable person. We decided that she was because there was nothing to indicate otherwise. Looking back on all the behaviors in which Dan had engaged over the final month, it seemed reasonable for someone to be in substantial fear, despite the fact that she had not been a victim of previous physical abuse. If you had asked me this same question three weeks earlier, I'm not sure I could have made that jump. As we went through the analytical process of what it really meant, however, it slid into place like a key in a lock.

We moved on to Element C, but we didn't need to spend a great deal of time on it. It seemed clear that fear was the modus operandi that Dan had purposefully employed to get Beth to come back. Not only did we believe he should have known it would cause fear in Beth, we believed it was, in all likelihood, his intent.

In all, it took us about three hours to resolve the stalking charge, which was much longer than any of us had expected. We had worked very well together, had given the defendant every reasonable benefit of doubt, and had reached a conclusion.

After three hours, we took a hand ballot: twelve guilty, zero not guilty. We were unanimous. We had just agreed that Dan Kutz was guilty of stalking.

It was a bizarre feeling. I had just spent three hours thinking, talking, listening, writing, reading, and analyzing. The result of that was incredibly intense. All I knew of my own personal accord about this man was that he was quiet and calm. He showed little by way of emotion one way or the other. He had smiled occasionally, when something funny had happened or when his children walked by to testify.

Again, I was stricken with the inevitable reality of this man being a father, a brother, a son. His children had said good things about him, as had his sister and his priest. I felt that what we had just done was right, but that didn't make it any easier. Because there was now one certainty for the first time in this repugnant experience; it was no longer possible for Dan Kutz to walk out of that courtroom a free man.

TWENTY-FOUR

It's hard to convict someone of murder when there is absolutely no physical evidence to demonstrate that the victim is even dead. Not only do you not know, but it's truly possible you never will. Other than a missing person, there was nothing but circumstantial evidence piled high and wide.

One doesn't want to reward someone just because he might be smart enough, lucky enough, or both, to commit the perfect crime. This was the most intense issue I had ever faced, one with which the entire jury wrestled during every single one of those eighteen days. It is an issue with which I continue to wrestle, to this very day.

Up to this point, we had worked very well together. Some people talked a great deal and others did not, but that was to be expected. Most of the time someone could just start talking and it would work out okay. Other times, there were a number of people who wanted to talk simultaneously, and we would instinctually begin raising our hands, and James, our foreman, would call on us in turn.

There was some discussion about where to go next, but most people finally agreed with James and me: we should move to the murder charge. Even though we knew it would be the most difficult, the other two charges stemmed from this one. If we found him guilty of murder, it stood to reason that he lied to the police (obstruction of justice) and did something to ensure Beth's body would not be found (hiding a corpse). If we decided that he hadn't killed her, it would have a significant effect on our opinions regarding the other two charges.

I knew this was going to be hard. There are two components of first-degree murder:

A. *The defendant caused, or was a substantial factor in the cause of, Beth Kutz's death, and*

B. *The defendant had the intent to kill, with intent defined as:*

   The mental purpose to take the life of Beth Kutz, or

   An awareness that the conduct in which he was engaging was practically certain to cause the death of another human (in this case, Beth).

Element A was a cause-and-effect element. The cause was Dan's action. The effect was Beth's death. Element B did not require what I've always thought of as "premeditation." It did not require the intent to exist for any particular length of time before the act was committed or that the act be "brooded over, considered, or reflected upon for a week, a day, an hour, or even a minute." There need not be any appreciable time between the formation of the intent and the act.

There must be a "mental purpose" or an "awareness that the conduct is practically certain to result in death," formed in the instant preceding the act or sometime before and which continued to exist during the time of the act.

It got even worse: we had to find intent to kill, but jury instructions told us that we could not look into a person's mind to find out his intent. We were flabbergasted as to how we'd even begin to find "mental purpose" or "awareness" without looking into someone's mind. Thankfully, we could consider Dan's statements or conduct that might indicate state of mind. But we were still not supposed to look into his mind. These requirements seemed to contradict each other. It was yet another obstacle whose construction I couldn't fathom. Finally, we did not need to find motive, nor was it necessary for the State to prove that there was one.

All of this required, of course, that we decide beyond a reasonable doubt that Beth Kutz was indeed dead. I'd been struggling with this for over two weeks and there I was, in the deliberation room, with much stronger beliefs but absolutely no certainty. I have never felt so pained and stressed in my entire life. We were about to decide whether another human being, one whom we now felt we knew very well, would spend the rest of his life in prison. I could imagine few things that would trouble me more than this. I again asked that everyone remember the significance of this and be patient, ensuring that everyone in the room was comfortable with the decision we reached before we left. As the words were leaving my mouth, it began to dawn on me that, whatever happened, I would never be comfortable with this.

I was immensely thankful that we had been sent to Deliberation Room 2. I couldn't imagine what it would have been like in room one, where Jessica, Rick, and I had laughed so hard that our sides hurt. This room was a new beginning, a fresh start, just like deliberations. It was exactly what we needed. I whispered a quiet "thank you" to whoever had made this decision, unaware as they undoubtedly had been.

It was clear that the first thing we had to do was decide whether or not Beth was indeed dead. All else stemmed from this. The prosecution had made a huge case for the fact that Beth could not have disappeared of her own accord. They had proven she hadn't taken public transportation or withdrawn any money. They told us about domestic intervention shelters, the armed forces, the witness protection program, passports, her social security account, and her last paycheck. All indicated that something had happened to Beth. They brought in character witness after character witness to tell us how much Beth loved her family, her friends, and her job. They told us about her activities with the church and her infatuation with her new boyfriend, Greg. Her family described how close they all were to her. Friend after friend had gotten up and testified that Beth had been their friend for years and had *always* been there for them. Since July 27th, Beth had missed Thanksgiving and Christmas, numerous school events, friends' birthdays, and the birthdays of both her children, Jacob and Jennifer. These were things she had never missed in the past. Witness after witness reiterated the same basic theme: it just wasn't possible that Beth disappeared of her own accord.

It didn't take us long to unanimously agree that something terrible had happened to Beth. There were doubts raised by the defense, but none of us believed they were "reasonable." It basically came down to this: Kitsie was watching the kids that day. When Kitsie watched the kids, Ellen picked them up when she finished work at 1 p.m. On July 27th, Ellen wanted to get some things done around the house, so Beth had asked Kitsie if she could keep the kids longer, until 4 p.m. when Beth could come pick them up. Kitsie said sure. At 3 p.m., Beth called Ellen and said she'd be home in half an hour so they could drive to Kitsie's together and get the kids. "If I'm not home in thirty minutes, come looking for me," were the last words Ellen Maier ever heard from her daughter. The children were never picked up.

The prosecution made a rock-solid case that this simply would not have happened had Beth been okay. We were confident and unanimous, albeit incredibly saddened, by the fact that there was no way Beth had disappeared of her own accord. We were confident that she was dead.

This was astounding. In all this time, I had never consciously thought about Beth being dead. I didn't really understand how it was possible. We were not supposed to draw conclusions about the case until deliberations, and it seemed clear to me as I sat there and admitted to myself that Beth was definitely dead that I had passed that test. The problem was that, in many ways, the realization made her death real for the first time. Even the maps and the 911 tape, which had pounded home the terrible reality that something tragic had occurred, had somehow not caused me to actually think about Beth being dead. After all this preparation, I still wasn't ready for that. I knew Beth very well at this point. I knew her likes and dislikes, and felt very strongly that she had been a good person. I had wanted so badly for her to walk into that courtroom, but it was not ever going to happen. I was overcome by a tsunami of sadness, but by now I was growing accustomed to that.

Once we reached this conclusion, we began dissecting Element A (the defendant caused, or was a substantial factor in causing, Beth Kutz's death), but we encountered another obstacle. Because we were in Dane County and Dan had been charged here, the murder had to have taken place in Dane County. We did not believe that Beth had died in Dane County, however, and were extremely concerned. We sent another question to the judge.

> *If we determine that the defendant is guilty of the intentional homicide of Beth Kutz, but we cannot determine beyond a reasonable doubt that it occurred in Dane County, can a guilty verdict still be returned?*

Kurt returned quite a bit later with our answer:

> *See supplemental instruction on venue.*

The supplemental instruction was attached:

> *If the offense is committed in, or against a vehicle, the trial may be held in* any *county through which the vehicle has passed or in the county where the travel began or ended. Therefore, you must be satisfied beyond a reasonable doubt that the vehicle involved in*

> *this offense (the Jeep Cherokee) passed through Dane County or that the travel began or ended in Dane County. Additionally, if the act causing death is in one county, and the death occurs in another, then the trial may be held in either county.*

Once we determined that the county lines were not a barrier to the act, we had to find that Dan caused, or was a substantial factor in the cause of, Beth's death. We discussed Bob Kaiser's powerful questions during his closing statement: "Who else?" and "Why else?" If a stranger had done the deed, if this were, in fact, some random act of violence, then why would someone go to the trouble of hiding the body? Why wouldn't the person just dispose of her on a roadside somewhere? No one but Dan would know the length to which this family would go to find her. It was a good point, and it hung heavily around us.

Other than this theory, which we deemed entirely valid, we focused solely on facts and what we knew:

- Dan had been following Beth to work with increasing regularity.
- Beth had said on the day she disappeared, "If I'm not home in thirty minutes, come looking for me."
- Beth, and at least three other people, had seen Dan driving around Demco (Beth's workplace) on multiple occasions that day.
- Dan, after being noticed in his own car, had driven to his brother's to switch to a car that people would not associate with him.

- Dan parked his brother's car on the side of the road Beth used to get home, less than an hour before she was to get off work.

- Dan had somehow gotten into Beth's Jeep as she was driving home from work that day.

- The vice-president of their bank, someone that knew both of them, testified that he'd seen Beth driving the Jeep onto the 180-acre property that afternoon.

These facts made us very suspicious, but they were not enough. In the end, there were really three things that made us certain that Dan was responsible:

- The key to Dan's brother's car (a Mercury Cougar) was found by detectives at the 180-acre property. We knew Beth had been there from the testimony of the bank vice-president.

- Dan's story to detectives in the early morning hours of July 28, 2000 was that he and Beth had driven off together around 3:15 p.m., and after reconciling, she had left him around 9:00 p.m. His "theory" was that something happened to Beth after 9:00 p.m.

- Beth never called her mother, whom she must have known was now frantically looking for her daughter. And Beth never called Kitsie, who had already agreed to

> watch Jennifer and Jacob for three hours longer than usual. If she had been able, there was simply no way that Beth would not have called.

To us, there was absolutely *no* way that Beth Kutz was still alive at 9:00 p.m. on the night of July 27th. And Dan Kutz *said* he was with her that entire time until 9:00 p.m. His comments, combined with the key at the 180, were all it took. He simply had to have done it—no other alternative was feasible. Once we decided that, it was pretty clear that whatever took place had happened in Dane County. The travel had originated near Demco, which is in Dane County, and had concluded in the Meriter parking lot, which is also in Dane County. The venue question was no longer an issue.

Dan had killed Beth. We were sure, and our vote was unanimous.

TWENTY-FIVE

After we voted, a collective hush descended on our small room. We had just decided that this man, Dan Kutz, had killed his wife. It seemed there was no going back now. I wanted to make sure we were all completely comfortable with this decision, so I reminded everyone that this essentially ended the issue of the Jeep sightings. Effectively, it said we either don't believe or don't care about Dan Kutz's primary defense strategy. A juror asked why. I explained by saying, "The entire defense is based on the Jeep sightings on Friday and Saturday. If we decide he killed her, then the Jeep sightings no longer have any relevance to the remainder of our discussion. Are you all sure that you are comfortable with that?" At least a couple people raised their hands to indicate that they were not. Some people were growing increasingly impatient with this process, but several of us thought we owed it to Dan, to our commitment to each other, and, most importantly, to the truth, to discuss it further.

We pored back through our notes and found every single witness who mentioned seeing the Jeep. Rick and I wrote them into a chart on the blackboard with the column headings:

Name
Time
Place seen
Direction headed
Meriter link?
Credible?

We filled in the chart for Thursday, July 27th and felt confident that the Jeep was parked in the Meriter lot that night. The only Thursday witnesses to see the Jeep were two women who'd had a great deal to drink that night. Because three people had seen the Jeep in the Meriter lot early Friday morning, we chose to discount the sighting by the two women as a mistake.

The only Jeep sighting witness the defense brought forward in whom we had real faith was a sweet, humorous man who lived next door to the Jeep's owner, Diane (Beth's friend, who had lent her the vehicle). We trusted him because he knew the Jeep and the DIDIS license plate. Even though the defense was clearly trying to lead us in a particular direction, the time the witness claimed to have seen the Jeep *could have* worked with a timeline of guilt. In fact, if he'd been delayed by a train on his way home from work that day, the timing of his sighting would have fit perfectly with everything else that the prosecution claimed had happened that day.

We continued into Friday. The first three people to see the Jeep on the *road* Friday all worked at Meriter or had been in the Meriter parking lot that morning. Were they sure they'd seen it on the road and not in the parking lot? Already three others had testified to seeing the Jeep in the Meriter parking lot. We decided, being as these three all worked at Meriter, they *could* have seen the Jeep in the lot and just *thought* they had seen it on the road.

Saturday was more of the same. There were questions and contradictions, even among defense witnesses. It seemed like a less-than-perfect strategy to present us with witnesses that contradicted each other (some witnesses saw the Jeep on different sides of town at approximately the same time). Because the defense essentially discredited some of their own witnesses, they made it easier for us to discredit the others.

In the end, it didn't matter at all. An interesting thing had happened that morning. On our way to the courthouse from the hotel, we'd noticed a green Jeep Cherokee with personalized plates. The license plate read FORSNO and we had noticed it because a personalized green Jeep had been, to say the least, on our minds a great deal lately.

So there we were at deliberations, reviewing all the Jeep sightings on the blackboard and discussing their individual meanings and significance. Suddenly, someone turned and asked me what the license plate had been on the Jeep we'd seen that morning. I could not remember—I racked my brain up and down and left and right and still couldn't remember. No one else could either. Here was a green Jeep Cherokee with personalized plates—the most important piece of our existence for three weeks—that a group of us had seen and talked about *just that morning*, and we couldn't remember the plates.

It was shocking how quickly our memories had faded. We finally remembered, however, after someone recalled "F.. O..R… something." Having joked about foreheads and foreskins at the time of the sighting, we finally remembered. Then we imagined what it would be like if, instead of us thinking about it four hours later, we'd thought of it four days later, or even just one day later, after seeing a picture of "4sno" or "forsnow" on the local news on a car that had absolutely no personal meaning or connection. How could we be exactly sure of what the license plate had said or how it was spelled? Would we have testified under oath to what we'd seen? We all agreed that we probably would have, and we'd have been wrong.

One juror summed it up quite nicely: "The Jeep stops here." Truly, it did.

It was an unbelievable twist of fate that had put us in the right place at the right time to see the green Jeep Cherokee with the "FORSNO" plates that morning. We'd been commenting on personalized plates constantly for three weeks. We'd looked for them, talked about them, unanimously agreed that we would *never* get them, and conversed on meanings whenever we'd seen one. But we'd never seen them on a green Jeep Cherokee.

To see that seemingly random vehicle at all during the trial would have been beyond belief. To see it on the first morning of deliberations, only a few hours before we were going to discuss the importance of that very thing, was mind-boggling. And though the Jeep sightings ultimately played only a peripheral role in our deliberations, the sighting of "our" Jeep that morning played a critical role in our discussion of its importance and the amount of weight we would give it.

"Draw upon your own observations and experiences," the judge had told us. We needed some help, and the universe had very graciously accommodated our needs.

Ultimately, the defense's Jeep-sighting testimony didn't matter. We decided and agreed upon the following:

- The key to the Cougar proved that Dan had been at the 180-acre property. The bank vice president's testimony proved that Beth had been with him.
- The Jeep was in the Meriter Hospital parking lot on Thursday night and Friday morning, which fit with a presumption of guilt.
- We strongly believed that the power of suggestion was at work here and that most of the Jeep witnesses, while meaning well, were likely mistaken.
- We didn't care whether the witnesses were mistaken or not. We decided that it was possible, albeit unlikely, that Dan had an accomplice drive the Jeep around town on Friday and Saturday to confuse people. Even so, all that mattered was that the Jeep was parked in the ramp on Thursday night, even if it went somewhere else the next day.

- The defense had asked us how we could discredit their witnesses and sightings, but not the two key Jeep witnesses of the prosecution (Faga and Snorek). I made this point during deliberations: "I don't care whether Snorek and Faga are credible or not. You take them out of the picture and I'm still convinced that Dan killed her on the night of the 27th, hid her corpse, and drove to the Meriter ramp in Madison." Everyone agreed.

- The Jeep was completely, one-hundred percent, devoid of fingerprints, save one, as if the vehicle had been wiped clean and one spot had been missed. That lone fingerprint belonged to the defendant.

We believed unanimously that the Jeep was parked at the Meriter ramp on Thursday night, July 27th, and Friday morning, July 28th. That, combined with Dan's claim that he'd been with Beth until 9 p.m. and the finding of the key at their 180-acre property, was all we needed to believe that Dan was responsible for his wife's death.

Our search for truth required that we take two completely different paths: one followed Dan and Beth, the other the Jeep sightings. Both ended with the same conclusion. We voted again. It was unanimous; we all believed that Dan Kutz had killed Beth on the night of July 27th.

Unfortunately, we had only tackled two of the three requirements. Beth was dead and Dan had killed her. This was a critical start, but it had taken us a long time and a lot of work to take what amounted to a few small steps on a long journey. We still had intent, and thus still had a long way to go.

Twenty-six

Earlier, during deliberations, several jurors had voiced their opinion that the hard part of this charge was going to be Element A (cause) and the easy part Element B (intent). If we decided Dan was responsible, intent was a given. I disagreed immediately, saying that I thought the opposite was true. There was no question in my mind: establishing intent was going to be a struggle.

We didn't even know where to start on intent. Carefully we read its definition, attempting to grasp the meaning, and then read it again and again. And again.

> *"Mental purpose."*
> *"Aware that he is engaging in conduct that is practically certain to result in death."*

What did this mean? We had been told that we were not to go into Dan's mind, but how on earth were we supposed to determine the legitimacy, or even the most remote possibility, of those two phrases without doing so? It bordered on ludicrous, and we were lost right from the start. I came up with a strategy: we would write on our chalkboard everything we could think of that would lean in favor of, or against, intent. Eventually, we had quite a list:

- Dan had forced himself into Beth's Jeep. Why had he done this? If he just wanted to talk, why hadn't he done so under different, less ominous, circumstances? Maybe he knew she wouldn't talk to him, and forcing her to talk would have been the only way he could get her attention.
- "If you leave me, you'll never see your kids grow up." We had listened to so many people testify they'd heard Dan say this that we could almost imagine it carved in wood and hanging above their front door. Who knows what it meant—maybe that Dan would take the kids and move away. Maybe something worse.
- "They'll bury all four of us on the hill." We had heard this quote with even greater frequency. But what did it really mean? Did it mean he'd kill her? If one assumes that, then why wouldn't one assume it meant that he'd kill himself and the children, too? Most of us believed it meant nothing of the sort and was more likely tied to the financial ruin Dan was expecting if they were to lose the land.
- Anger over Greg Stahl. It was clear that Dan had been

angry and jealous. He was a controlling, manipulative man; of that, there was no doubt. And his wife was cheating on him. As if this weren't enough, Greg Stahl had to add insult to injury the fateful day of the 27th, by screaming at Dan, "Get a life, buddy." There's no doubt Dan had been rattled, but there's a gulf of difference between anger and *murderous* anger.

- The key to the Cougar was found deep in the 180-acre property. If Dan had just wanted to talk to Beth, and didn't have "naughty thoughts" (as Rick called them), why did he drive all the way to their 180-acre property? And why did he drive so far into the land, at least a mile from the highway? Why not just park closer to the front entrance? My thought was, why not? Maybe that farther area was where they had always parked (there is a cement slab there that could be used for parking) and it had just seemed natural to go there. It was a good question though, and we interpreted it several different ways.

- "You can have sex with them and they still leave." This is what Dan told his brother later that night after the police had dropped him off at John Kutz's house. What did this mean? Because of the semen and vaginal fluid stains found on the back of Dan's jeans later that night, we believed Beth and Dan had had intercourse (we knew that DNA evidence could have been present from a previous encounter), even though it had been clear that Beth was still going to leave him. But why did Dan make the above comment to John and then tell the police later that night that he and Beth had reconciled?

- Dan saw Ellen, Jennifer, and Jacob that morning. He hadn't waved. Why hadn't he greeted his own children? Was he already gone at that point? Was he planning and already focused on what had to be done?

- July 27th was the last day for the redemption period on the 180-acre property. It had been one year since foreclosure, and this 180-acre parcel of land that meant so much to Dan was going to fall under the bank's control that afternoon, later to be sold by Sheriff's auction. Why had everything happened on this day? Coincidence?

- Escalation of violent behavior. I think a number of us had a hard time with this because Dan had never hit Beth before. (Beth had told her family everything, and we'd heard about the emotional and verbal abuse from every one of them. If it had come to blows, we would probably have known about it.) Usually, in domestic cases, there is an escalation of physical violence that demonstrates some sort of pattern. In this case, no physical violence was evident, which made it difficult for us to make the jump from never hitting Beth to killing her. But the emotional and mental abuses, as well as the violent tendencies, were increasing in frequency. Dan had thrown the telephone. He had blocked Beth's car and yelled at her in front of the children. He had locked Beth in the bathroom. He had followed her with much greater frequency. Beth was frightened. It was a long and winding path to get from there to murder, but it did seem plausible.

- Beth was visibly upset on July 27th when she left Demco. Numerous witnesses testified that Beth had been in a good mood that morning. From about 1 p.m., however, several witnesses testified to a marked change in her attitude. We believed she talked to Dan around that time and then became very upset.

- All of Beth's pictures and a blanket were found in the trunk of the Cavalier. The Cavalier was Beth and Dan's car, the one in which Dan had originally been spotted before he switched to his brother's Cougar. Why were all these things in the trunk? The prosecution theorized it was Dan's trump card to get Beth to talk to him, to listen to whatever it was he had to say. Although plausible, we didn't agree. We thought it more likely that Dan was trying to hold on to something, something that he could ensure Beth couldn't get. He was a desperate man. Whatever the reason, it was clear that Dan had thrown those things into the trunk, and it didn't seem his actions were part of some grand plan for reconciliation. But we didn't completely rule it out either.

- Switching from the Cavalier to the Cougar. Again, was this an act of a desperate man that had something planned for that day and was intent on ensuring that it not go awry? All we jurors knew was that Dan had been desperate and that July 27th was an important day.

Otherwise, once Greg Stahl spotted him and called the police, Dan might have gone home and tried again on Friday, July 28th.

- Hanging out and waiting for Beth. Why had Dan been sitting in an unfamiliar car on the edge of the road where Beth would drive by? If he had wanted to talk to her, couldn't he have called her or visited her at work? Why wait there, hiding, and then sneak up on her? Again, this portended bad intentions.

- Beth had said to Ellen: "If I'm not home in thirty minutes, come looking for me." This statement was pretty significant to us. Why this day? What was she scared of? And if she had been okay later, why wouldn't she have called to let her family know that she was okay?

- Kelly (Dan's sister) to John (Dan's brother): "Let's go find Dan before something happens." This was significant to us as well. Even Dan's own family had been scared that he might do something. Did Kelly know something?

- Where were the knife and shovel that had been dangled a few times during the trial? We didn't know and, honestly, didn't really care. These were not essential elements for us, but we certainly believed they could have played a role.

We finished and spent long minutes staring at the list. Each of the quotes was discussed, each of the occurrences mulled over. We then analyzed each of the theories. Our ponderings quickly got us to Dan's state of mind. To anger and rage. To frustration and jealousy. To desperation. We conclusively and unanimously agreed that by that fateful afternoon and evening, Dan was a very desperate man.

But not necessarily murderous.

There are countless enraged, frustrated, jealous, and desperate people in the world. Only a slim, barely perceptible minority ever allow those emotions to escalate to murder. No single item on the list would have convinced us. Nor would two. But the list was long, and when all the items were taken in sum, it was extremely troubling. But again, it didn't get us to murder. At first.

We decided to take a vote. I was pretty sure that I wasn't the only one with doubts, but I didn't think there would be many. I remember guessing that we'd have three "not guilty" and nine "guilty." We still had a long way to go; things were just beginning. We voted: Four "guilty" and eight "not guilty."

I was shocked, for I couldn't believe so many of us had lingering doubts. Perhaps one or two of us—but eight? Twin emotions ran through me: I was simultaneously satisfied that people were really giving Dan the benefit of the doubt and scared as hell that we had such a long way to go.

We knew that Dan had killed Beth, but that wasn't enough. Frustration ruled the jury room—with ourselves, the process, and the prosecution for not giving us another choice. We sent another question to the judge:

If we feel that Kutz caused Beth's death, but are unsure of intent, beyond a reasonable doubt, is there a lesser homicide offense?

We knew what the answer would be before we even formed, much less penned, the question—but we wanted to be absolutely certain. Minutes later, the answer came back:

> *There is no lesser included offense contained in your instructions.*

In other words, we were stuck. There was no safety zone in which to find solace. It was all or nothing.

With all the work we had done and conclusions we had drawn, it may seem odd that our vote was so strongly against conviction. In actuality, however, we were neither voting *against* conviction nor were we voting "not guilty." We were saying, in that special way that only jurors could understand, "*I'm not ready yet*." There is a canyon between the former and the latter.

We needed to reach unanimity and I knew it was going to be a long, hard battle to get there. We were now in our eighteenth day of jury duty and the hours seemed to stretch to years. We were unbelievably exhausted, so far removed from simple comforts we used to take for granted: home-cooked meals, a relaxing evening, talking to friends on the phone, sleeping in our own beds, and spending time with our families.

And we were tired—tired of spending time together, tired of each other, and tired of hotels and bailiffs. But those things didn't really matter. What we were *really* tired of was murder. Dead and missing bodies. Blood and DNA. Orphaned children. Grieving brothers and fathers and mothers. Resolute, unending sadness. We were really tired of all the sadness.

We broke for the night at 10:30. We didn't make a sound the entire way back to the hotel, and everyone went immediately to sleep. It didn't help. We were just as exhausted when we filed back to deliberations at seven o'clock the next morning.

We knew we had to press on. The decision was made to record every single known step that Dan and Beth had taken that day (July 27, 2000), in chronological order on the chalkboard. Jessica would have been proud. Timmy would have been sick.

Several jurors had already decided Dan was guilty. By now, they were starting to wonder what our problem was and why the rest of us just couldn't just make up our minds. The pro-"guilty" folks had been frustrated earlier as we'd gone through the Jeep process. Now they were getting downright ornery. I don't think anyone walked into those deliberation rooms with his or her mind completely made up, but several jurors were darn close. They would have needed to hear something earth-shattering to change the opinions they had already formulated. In their minds, we were going through pointless exercises and unnecessary motions. However, the majority of the jury felt that we owed it to Dan and the truth to ensure that no stone went unturned.

We began to examine our notebooks and recreate every known detail about July 27, 2000. We started with morning. We began with the assumption that Beth went to work at 6 a.m. We knew she'd been changing her work times in order to avoid Dan, who had been following her with increasing regularity. A friend first saw her as she walked into Demco at 6:30 that morning. Beth's mother and the kids saw Dan driving the opposite direction that morning as they headed to Kitsie's.

There were Beth sightings on breaks at work that day. There was Greg's encounter with Dan, in which he told Dan to "Get a life, buddy" and then called the police. There was Dan changing cars. There was Beth paying her mother for babysitting. There was Beth's change of mood about 1 p.m. There was Beth's phone call to her mother, "If I'm not home in thirty minutes, come looking for me."

We went through every witness and read each testimony, each cross-examination and each rebuttal. We replayed the entire day in our heads, analyzing gaps and irregularities. We wrote every single activity or sighting on the blackboard, similarly to how we had organized the Jeep sightings list. Tiny letters covered the board, were crossed out, and were moved. It took us hours. The "already-decideds" were growing increasingly impatient and frustrated. The rest of us were quickly catching up. It was tedious, repetitive, and exasperating.

We stared at our list and discussed it, but it didn't us get very far. We looked at each other with a great deal of anguish.

Then we gave up.

TWENTY-SEVEN

We decided to switch over and address the other two charges. It seemed they would both be easier and would give us all something to agree on. We started with "hiding a corpse." There were two elements to this count:

A. *Hiding a corpse.*

B. *Hiding a corpse with the intent to conceal a crime or to avoid apprehension, prosecution, or conviction.*

I did not understand Element B; it seemed redundant. I could not conceive of any circumstance that would allow someone to be guilty of A and not B. Nonetheless, we didn't think this was much of an issue. We had already decided that Dan had killed Beth. No one had found Beth, and Dan had not said a word. It stood to reason that he had hidden the corpse, with the clear intent to conceal a crime and avoid apprehension, prosecution, *and* conviction.

With no discussion, we voted unanimously: Guilty.

We had now convicted Dan Kutz of two charges: stalking and hiding a corpse. The penalties for his crime, and thus the severity of what we were doing, were starting to grow exponentially.

We moved on to the charge of "obstruction of justice." For some unfathomable reason, this charge applied to only one officer, Garth Blake, the DeForest police officer who had first picked up Dan, walking shirtless and shoeless on the side of Highway CV just north of Packers Avenue. We were mystified as to why this charge was limited to only one police officer, because there was absolutely no doubt that Dan had obstructed detectives Heimerl, Pertzborn, and Wormett later that night. These detectives had talked to Dan specifically regarding Beth's disappearance. If we had already found him guilty of killing her and hiding her corpse, it was an absolute certainty that Dan had "misled the officers who, in official capacity, were trying to perform their duties." That's obstruction of justice. That's guilty.

But the three detectives were intentionally and specifically not included in the count. Why? They'd interviewed Dan in Dane County. They were members of the Deforest Police Department (which is in Dane County). There seemed to be no reason why only Officer Blake would be mentioned and included. We were frustrated and angry, but got down to business anyway.

There were four elements of this count:

A. *Dan knowingly gave false information (to Officer Blake).*

B. *The officer was doing an act in an official capacity.*

C. *The officer was doing an act with lawful authority.*

D. *Dan intended to mislead the officer in the performance of his or her duty.*

Officer Blake had been dispatched via 911 after a nurse at Meriter Hospital had called in to report a single male stumbling down the road, weaving on and off the shoulder and into the lane of oncoming traffic. Blake told us how he had stopped his police car on the shoulder, with lights flashing. He had been acting in official capacity and with lawful authority, so Elements B and C were satisfied.

Blake told us that Dan had just kept walking, right around the marked squad car. Officer Blake stopped him before he got very far. Blake told us how he had thought Dan was drunk, and that the shirtless man had crashed his car in a nearby field. Dan answered all Blake's questions politely and cooperatively, but offered little information. Dan told Blake that he'd been in a car with some guys, and that they had had a loud argument. He had been let off at the Stop-N-Go where, once inside, he'd realized he'd left his boots in their car.

"What kind of car?" Officer Blake had asked.

"I don't know," Dan had responded.

"Who were the people?"

"I don't know."

“What are their names?”

“I don’t know.”

“What type of car? What color?”

You get the idea. Most of us agreed that Dan was lying and therefore that Dan was guilty. If he had lied to Blake, he had obstructed justice. But I wasn’t convinced, and it was at that moment that the storm clouds began to form. I realized right then that it was going to be an increasingly vexatious battle from there on out. People had been impatient but had mostly contained it within frustrated grumbles and annoyed whispers. This was the first time true impatience, anger, and exhaustion bubbled to the surface and were publicly voiced. I was frustrated and worried when we broke for lunch.

We started eating and talking about non-trial things. This was heavy stuff, so lunch was a welcome break indeed. But after a few minutes, our conversation turned back to the subject of obstruction of justice. We were all in the room, so we decided to continue the discussion over our food.

We reviewed all of Dan’s *known* lies from that night:

- Dan told Blake he had been with strangers in their car. Later that night, he told the detectives that he had been in the Jeep with Beth. At least one of those statements was a lie.

- Dan told Blake that he’d left his boots in the strangers’ car. Later that night, he told the detectives that he’d left the boots in the Jeep.

- Dan told Blake that he was walking home. Later that night, when the detectives questioned him, Dan told the officers that Beth had dropped him off at the Stop-N-Go and offered him a ride home. While leaning into the open window of the Jeep, Dan's response had been, "I'm walking home." Home was twenty-five miles away.

- Dan lied about which car was parked (he said the Cavalier, not the Cougar).

- Dan lied about where his brother's Cougar was parked.

- Dan switched stories about where Beth parked the Jeep at the Stop-N-Go. First it was in front of the Laundromat, against the curb. Once he found out that they would check the video camera, he changed his story to having parked in the gas islands.

- We were not sure, but Dan probably lied about having intercourse with Beth in the front seat of her Jeep (we figured that DNA or other evidence would have been found on the seat if this were the truth).

Another thing that puzzled us: Dan said that he and Beth had gone to the Stop-N-Go because they were hungry. Dinner at a Stop-N-Go? It's a gas station/convenience store. Also, it was at least five miles south of the park where Dan said that they had been. Beth's house, her parents' home, and the children were all north. It was the exact opposite direction.

These significant lies played a crucial role in our frame of mind and decision-making process. However, with regard to obstruction of justice, the big question related to the lies about the car versus the Jeep. Which had he been in?

Everyone was convinced that Dan was guilty of obstruction of justice—everyone except me. How did we know that the story he told Blake about being in the car was a lie? Dan had parked the Jeep at Meriter and had begun walking. While walking the seven miles from downtown Madison to the Stop-N-Go where he was next spotted, it's *possible*, albeit unlikely, that he had hitched a ride with some people unknown to him. How could we know that it wasn't what happened?

Even if it was a lie, how did it affect Officer Blake? Did it mislead him? From what? All he was doing was picking up a possibly drunk pedestrian to ensure his safety. How did anything Dan say, or not say, mislead Blake in the performance of his duties? If the detectives from later that night had been included in this charge, it would have been a no-brainer. We would have needed less than thirty seconds to find Dan guilty. I remember banging my fists on the table and wondering aloud on several occasions during this exchange, "Why the hell did they do this to us?"

Our instructions were quite explicit and I was intent on following them. This was frustrating for everyone. We knew that Dan had obstructed justice that night. There was no doubt in our minds. But the instructions very clearly restricted the charge to Blake. My fellow jurors had an easier time making the jump than I. People were definitely getting aggravated with me for holding out. I felt badly, but didn't care; their frustrations had to be put aside. I *needed* to be convinced. All of us were anxious, tired, and yearned to go home. I closed my eyes, took some deep breaths, and tried to relax.

I continued to ask the same questions about whether or not Dan had really lied to Blake, over and over again, but the answers I got were unsatisfactory. We knew the second story about Beth and the Jeep was a lie. If you tell a truth, and then tell a new "truth" that is a lie, does that automatically discount the first truth? I couldn't say for sure. Everyone else felt that it did. Plus, people agreed that because Beth *was* missing, Dan had misled Blake, even though Blake wasn't even looking for her. To agree with the others, I felt I would have to use a broader definition of the officer's "performance of duties."

Nothing was clear-cut, except for the fact that Dan *had* obstructed the detectives later that night. Maybe he had lied to Blake as well. There was no doubt that he definitely changed his story later that night, which certainly implied the original story had not been the truth. In addition, wasting Blake's time to get a free ride to his brother's with the thought of freeing himself from further disturbance that night implied obstruction as well.

I kept asking questions, playing devil's advocate, pointing out holes in each answer and argument. Each person was focused on the one or two aspects that had led to the belief that Dan was guilty. These aspects were different for each juror, but none of the elements, taken alone, convinced me. I decided to take them all together: all the lies, all the intentional misdirection, all the lack of cooperation. It was much harder than I'd thought it would be, but if I looked at everything that happened, I finally decided I could get to guilt.

After we finished lunch, I tried to relax by hacking with James and Rick. It was mindless, and therefore consoling, but it wasn't satisfying. I think Rick and I were thinking the same thing: it felt strange without Jessica. There was no joy in our hacking, and it wasn't long before we were all locked back in the deliberation room. We took another vote. Our lunchtime discussion had been enough to help me make my decision, but I was still concerned. I was beginning to think that I would never be comfortable with the decisions I was making, but I hoped I could at least live with them.

When we took the vote, my hand went up slowly, but it went up, and it was finally unanimous: Dan Kutz was guilty of obstruction of justice. Three counts decided, three "guilty" verdicts.

It was a very odd feeling. A man's fate had rested freely and comfortably in our hands, like a marble we had rolled around in our palms, for three weeks. Our hands were beginning to clench, locking a man's future ever more tightly inside. We now knew that Dan Kutz was going to spend a lot of time behind bars, regardless of what we decided next.

TWENTY-EIGHT

After the vote, we immediately dove back into "intent" to decide if Dan had had "mental purpose" and "awareness of conduct practically certain to result in death."

I approached our helpful blackboard and started writing a list of anything and everything that would demonstrate or deflate intent. We developed a timeline based on notes, testimony, and memory. We then analyzed every single element of our list, as well as the details that made the segue from one event to the next possible.

When we finished, here is what the blackboard looked like:

No.	Activity	Time
1	Dan and Beth at 51 and Grinde Rd	3:20 PM
2	Dan and Beth together at 180 acre property	3:35 PM
3	Faga sees Dan at S curve on Hwy J	4:15 PM
4	Dan goes to house on J (a guess)	4:20 PM?

5	Purse dropped on Hwy 12 (a guess)	5:40 PM?
6	Snorek sighting on Mineral Point	5:55 PM
7	Snorek sees Jeep at Meriter	6:15 PM
8	Dan is videotaped at Stop-N-Go	9:15 PM
9	Dan is picked up by the police near the VFW	11:00 PM

No.	Time	Distance	Activity	Feasibility
1 to 2	15 min.	9 miles by car	Dan makes Beth drive there	feasible
2 to 3	40 min.	9 miles by car	Intercourse and Dan kills Beth	tight, but feasible
3 to 4	~5 min.	4.5 miles by car	Dan drives, Beth dead in back	feasible
4 to 5	80 min.	19.7 miles by car	Dan disposes of Beth's body	tight, but feasible
5 to 6	15 min.	8.3 miles by car	Throws purse; on Min. Pt Rd.	feasible
6 to 7	20 min.	5.5 miles by car	Dan drives to Meriter	feasible
7 to 8	180 min.	7.9 miles by foot	Dan walks to Stop-N-Go	feasible
8 to 9	105 min.	2.5 miles by foot	Dan walks north on CV	feasible

Once our timeline was complete, we began to analyze and scrutinize the details trapped within each piece:

Number 1: We took a guess at the time, but we knew that Beth had left work at 3:15 p.m. We were assuming that it took her approximately five minutes to get into the Jeep and drive to the corner where we knew Dan was waiting to get into the Jeep. We knew this because the Cougar was later found at that exact spot.

Number 2: The bank vice-president was pretty confident about the time he saw Beth in the Jeep, turning into the 180-acre property. We assumed that Dan was with her because his key to the Cougar was later found there. Also, why else would Beth drive there when her mother and children were waiting?

Number 3: The time that Curt Faga spotted Dan, driving maniacally" at the S curve on Highway J, just north of the Kutz house. Faga testified that he "remembered the eyes."

Number 4: The prosecution theorized that Dan went to the house on J to get the shovel. We weren't sure we believed that. Either way, there was no evidence or testimony to that effect, so we indented the time and added a question mark, indicating that it was merely a guess and not a fact.

Number 5: For the purposes of fitting a timeline, we guessed on this one, too. No one saw the Jeep or Dan at this time, and the purse was not found until three months later. Working backward from Number 6 (Snorek testimony) and looking at the maps, we guessed at the time (about 5:40 p.m.) that Dan would have been in the area where the purse would later be found.

Number 6: Snorek testified that at this time, she spotted the Jeep on Mineral Point Road, just east of the Beltline, a few miles south of where the purse would later be found. It was the first direct evidence of the Jeep we had since Number 3, the Faga sighting.

Number 7: This is when Snorek saw the Jeep in the Meriter lot and wondered how it beat her there. She testified that the Jeep was driving very fast and cutting people off, so we were never quite sure why she was surprised that it had beat her to Meriter.

Number 8: This is when Dan was caught on a security camera videotape at the Stop-N-Go on the northeast side of Madison. The time stamp on the video showed us the date and time.

Number 9: This is the time that Officer Blake found Dan near the VFW, walking along the side of the road without shirt or shoes.

Of the nine activities on the timeline, only numbers 4 and 5 were guesses. The rest were based on direct evidence that was presented during the trial. Once we finished, we began looking *between* the time frames to make sure they worked. This was the "feasibility" column of the chart.

1 to 2: Dan was now in the Jeep, and had somehow coerced Beth to drive to the 180-acre property. It was a nine-mile drive on a county highway made in fifteen minutes, which we deemed feasible.

2 to 3: We included ten minutes of driving time to cover nine miles, which left thirty minutes for Dan and Beth to have intercourse and for Dan to kill her. This was tight and made us slightly uncomfortable, but we all agreed that it certainly was feasible.

3 to 6: We estimated some time frames within this range (house on J and purse on Hwy 12), but decided they didn't really matter. One hour and forty minutes lay between the Faga sighting at 4:15 p.m. and the Snorek sighting at 5:55 p.m. According to the route laid out by the prosecution, which we believed was feasible, Dan would have needed to cover thirty-seven miles in this span. Assuming forty-five minutes of driving, Dan had almost an hour to hide Beth's body. Again, we agreed it was tight, but enough time.

However, and we discussed this at length, we did not believe that it was enough time for Dan to *bury* Beth, unless he had already dug a hole. Most of us did not believe that Dan had premeditated this and, therefore, did not believe that a hole had been dug. That left a body of water, and the majority of us felt that this scenario, given the time frame, was much more likely.

6 to 7: Twenty minutes for Dan to drive the 5.5 miles from Mineral Point Road to the Meriter Hospital ramp. This was plenty of time and, we all agreed, feasible.

7 to 8: A three-hour gap existed between "Dan sightings." It is almost eight miles to the Stop-N-Go where Dan was next seen. It was certainly possible for Dan to have gotten there by foot, and knowing that taxi cabs, buses, hitch-hiking, and even the story about the guys and the car were all very real possibilities, it became even more feasible.

8 to 9: Approximately one hour and forty-five minutes were available for Dan to cover 2.5 miles by foot between the Stop-N-Go and the location where Officer Blake picked him up. Again, it was altogether feasible.

We sat there, looking at the blackboard, proud of the sound analysis we had just completed. However, we knew we still had to dive deeper.

Once we had agreed on the timelines and their potential feasibility, we went back through the entire sequence and discussed all the things that could have happened. This was critical for us to begin to get to intent.

Dan had somehow gotten into Beth's Jeep. Again, we were not really sure how he had done this, but we were sure it happened. The prosecution's theory of Dan jumping out from behind the parked Cougar, angrily wielding a knife, madly rushing up to Beth's Jeep and forcing himself in, held absolutely no credibility with any of us. It seemed preposterous, and we found it quite condescending that they had even suggested it. We had several theories, but we'll probably never know the truth.

My theory was that Beth pulled up at Grinde Road and Hwy 51. She stopped at the stop sign. There was a black Cougar on the shoulder, but why would anyone think twice about that? The black Cougar belonged to Dan's brother, and Dan had already switched into it to ensure that Beth wouldn't recognize him. I figure she would have been at the stop sign for at least twenty seconds. That would have given Dan plenty of time to rise from beside the Cougar, walk to the Jeep, and let himself into the backseat. He would have been seated in the car in a matter of seconds, long before Beth would even have realized what had happened.

Dan coerced or forced Beth to drive to the 180-acre property. Beth had already told her mother to come looking for her if she was not home in thirty minutes. Kitsie had already agreed to watch the kids three hours longer than usual. There was simply no way Beth would have driven to the 180 unless Dan was forcing or coercing her to do so. We trusted the bank vice-president who, on his way to play some golf, saw Beth driving the Jeep into the entrance of the property. We assumed that Dan was in the back of Jeep, probably crouched down behind Beth, or maybe the bank vice-president just missed him.

Beth and Dan drove well into the 180 and had sexual intercourse. Many jurors believed that Dan already had considered doing something terrible because there would be no reason to drive all the way into the silage pit (the paved parking area), which was located at least a half mile into the property. I disagreed, figuring it was nothing more than their typical parking spot. Nonetheless, we knew they went that far, because that's where the search team found the key to the Cougar later that weekend—on the pavement barely visible beneath some purple wildflowers.

Dan's pants, when collected as evidence later that night, showed semen and vaginal fluid stains, so we were pretty confident that they had sex. Beth had told her mother, "It makes me sick when he touches me," so we figured it was not consensual. But Dan was not charged with rape or sexual assault, so this was not an issue we discussed. However, we believed that Dan, at the very least, had put some strong emotional—or even physical—pressure on Beth to have intercourse with him.

We were left only to guess what happened next. Somehow, we surmised, *Dan must have become enraged.* In our hypothetical vision, Beth finally told Dan that she was leaving him and that it was over, that there was no hope for reconciliation, that they were going to lose the land, and there was absolutely nothing he could do about it. It was our presumption that Beth said something that had enraged Dan and tipped an already desperate man over the edge.

Sometime between five seconds and five minutes later, *Beth ended up dead.* Of course we had no idea how. We discussed certain plausible methods: strangling, beating, smothering. All of these spelled intent, given the second part of the definition: "Awareness that conduct in which he is engaging is practically certain to cause her death." One need not premeditate a murder. One must only have the aforementioned awareness, and one must only have this awareness for one second prior to the death and continuing through the actual death itself. It needn't be a day, an hour, or even a minute. Thus, we quickly decided that there were certain activities in which Dan *could* have engaged that would clearly spell intent.

The problem for me was this: I couldn't get out of my mind the very real possibility of the following scenario. Beth starts walking toward the Jeep, maybe saying something like "Dan, I have to go get the kids." Dan gets angry and pushes or shoves or grabs at her. Beth falls, hits her head on the Jeep or a rock in the silage pit, and dies. This would, in all likelihood, have been an accident, which in turn would imply a very troubling conclusion: no intent and no guilt.

Either way, Dan lost it at that point and carried a dead or dying Beth *to the back of the Jeep.* Even if it had been an accident, which it could have been, we could all see how Dan would panic and pretend he didn't do it. Her family already didn't trust him; even his own family didn't trust him completely. After his increasingly violent episodes and the stalking, if Beth died, everyone would automatically assume that he'd killed her on purpose.

Next, he went somewhere and hid her body. The prosecution theorized that he went back to their house on Highway J to get the shovel. This fit in with the Faga sighting of the Jeep just north of their house. We didn't know if he had actually gone into the house or not; most of us harbored serious doubts. Dan knew how close Beth was to her family. There were certain places they would look, and the house would be one of the most obvious. It would be risky to go there.

The prosecution also theorized that Dan buried the body. Based on our timeline, we didn't see how that could work out, unless he had already dug a hole. Since most of us did *not* believe that Dan had intended to kill her prior to driving to the 180, there would have been no reason to dig a hole.

Most of the jurors, including me, felt that Dan had hidden Beth in a body of water. There is water everywhere in that area, and Dan was a former trucker and hunter who had extensive knowledge of the local swamps, rivers, and lakes.

Dan drove west and south, the two safest directions to take him farther and farther away from his normal stomping grounds, and thus away from those areas where people would be searching for them. Somewhere on Highway 12, just north of Middleton, he threw Beth's purse out of the window, aiming for a small culvert beside the road. He just missed, and the highway clean-up crew found the purse three months later. He got off at Mineral Point Road and was spotted for the first time by Snorek. Fewer than twenty minutes later, the Jeep was parked in the Meriter Hospital ramp, and Dan was heading home on foot.

Later that night, after Dan had been picked up at his brother's house (the second time he'd been confronted by the police that night), three detectives started questioning him about Beth's whereabouts. He never said a word. He never asked if she was okay. He never suggested where she might be, or with whom. He never asked about his children or whether they were okay.

According to the police, throughout the hours upon hours of questioning about his wife of twelve years who was missing, Dan Kutz never showed one iota of emotion.

TWENTY-NINE

The four "guilty" votes in our intimate group had little to say during our deliberations about all this. But the "not guilty" jurors started questioning their positions. It started off relatively quietly. One juror asked, "Why did he drive all the way to the 180-acre property? And why did he drive so far in?"

Another added, "Why did he force himself into her car?"

Yet another: "Why did he pick that particular day? Why, once his car was spotted, did he switch cars? Was there some reason it had to be this day? What was he planning?"

I could see the tide turning quickly and tried to stem it. I wasn't sure I wanted that, but for some reason my instincts strongly supported my playing devil's advocate. I was so firmly entrenched in believing "innocent until proven guilty" that I needed more. More and more points, hypotheses, theories—all valid, all legitimate—were drowning out my voice. It took less than an hour for the barely perceptible ripple to become a wave and then a tsunami. We voted again: ten guilty, two not guilty.

I was shocked by the rapidity with which six people had changed their minds. There were a couple of people who probably already believed Dan was guilty. There was enough evidence to support that, so it shouldn't have come as a surprise.

The prosecution had never tied together a firm, solid theory on intent. They had made numerous implications, but never, not even in closing, came right out and drew us a picture. How could they? There was no body, so no one knew *how* Beth died. And without cause of death, how could the prosecution, with facts instead of guesses and innuendoes, demonstrate intent?

The tide had turned so fast I never saw it come in. Nonetheless, I remained unconvinced of Dan's guilt. To my pleasant and grateful surprise, I was not alone. One other juror stated her concerns, her *doubts*, and everyone focused their attention on her. It was a well-choreographed frontal assault, made more impressive because of its unrehearsed delivery. One would have never known. They hammered mercilessly away at her points and she withered beneath the assault.

It took fewer than twenty minutes to change her mind, and I was alone.

It had been a long three weeks, a very long trial. We'd been removed from our support systems and cut off from society. We'd been forced into near solitude with little reprieve. By this point, I was already a completely changed person, and knew for an absolute fact that I would never be the same again. I had heard and seen things I could have lived without and had harbored much apprehension and trepidation. But behind it all, high above all these doubts and worries, one fear had stood alone. It was so powerful that, despite my best efforts to keep it caged and somewhere out of view, it had always succeeded in reminding me of its presence. That which I had feared, above all else, had happened. We were deciding guilt on a first-degree murder charge. It was eleven to one, and I was the one.

THIRTY

I am only one; but still I am one. I cannot do everything,
but still I can do something;
I will not refuse to do something I can do.
Helen Keller

Is the defendant getting a fair shake when "mob rules" take over a jury? When people are so tired and so deprived that they are no longer willing to consider other opinions, other possibilities? How long can one expect people to go through such stress and emerge sane?

I think the jury process is flawed, but it is the best we have. But there is, however, one eventuality for which it is not well prepared—eleven to one.

There is no jury instruction for eleven to one. There is no how-to guide. Eleven to one is not good for the judicial process; it is the broken cog in the wheel. What options exist when eleven people have been deprived of their lives and their families for seventeen straight days and they are all in agreement about what to do next: that which will end everything and allow them, finally, to go home. Who could blame them for wanting to be finished? Who could fault them for focusing all this negative energy, blame, frustration, and anger for their current lot in life on the only person keeping them from achieving that dream: me.

I knew early on there would be no winners here; I didn't even bother debating, staring down, or whatever it usually took to get my point across. I had tried that move earlier and accomplished nothing more than watching seven "not guilty" votes turn into "guilty" votes. Although my opinion was not enough to sway the jury to "not guilty" (I'd already resigned myself to this fact), it was certainly enough to sway our decision in another direction: mistrial.

Looking around the table at the people with whom I'd spent so much time and for whom I had so much respect, who really wanted nothing more than to go home, I felt the pressure. It was intense.

Henry Fonda, in the movie "12 Angry Men," was able to change the tide because of his patience and fortitude. This was different. We were not strangers, and we'd been sequestered for three weeks. We wanted to go home. We had been eight to four in favor of not guilty. During the course of discussions and analysis, seven jurors had been swayed *away* from not guilty and were now firmly entrenched in the guilty camp.

There was no evidence or testimony remaining to call into question. We had already decided that Dan had killed his wife.

There was nothing, absolutely nothing, other than our sharp minds, careful analysis, and a bunch of educated guesses that would lead us to intent with no body or cause of death.

I felt I had no choices. How long is the "one" expected to hold out? How long was I expected to endure the glares and insults and intensity of the eleven others?

It was the most horrible experience of my life and it lasted for four grueling hours. I can't imagine what it would have been like had I needed three more days or another week. How long would the judge have forced me to withstand the pressure before hanging the jury and causing a mistrial?

It would have been a long time, probably at least a week, before the judge would have allowed that. It's hard to imagine how much time and money are invested in a trial of this length and severity. Already known for its long delays and backlogged dockets, there are few situations likely to cause the justice system to encourage more mistrials.

After this experience, I can say with absolute certainty that on countless occasions, the "one" has undoubtedly caved so quickly to the masses so as to negate any evidence he'd ever existed at all. Is that what we want from our jury system? Jurors who put aside their beliefs and their opinions because they are under more pressure than a volcano five seconds prior to eruption?

This was Dante's *Inferno*, and I was front and center.

THIRTY-ONE

The assault continued, but now was directed entirely toward me. It quickly descended down an even more desolate road. People scowled at me. People yelled and banged their fists on the table. People called me stupid. "How can you be so blind?" they asked. People who, less than four hours previous, had been completely and unabashedly uncertain and undecided, were now positive beyond any shadow of a doubt of Dan Kutz's guilt. "We see what you are saying; why can't you see what we are saying?" I was asked.

"I can see what you are saying," I replied. "Not only can I see it, but I see it as an entirely plausible explanation. But there are *other* possible explanations, too, and I can't just discount them." It was pretty clear that I was not getting through. Every comment I made, every hypothesis, every theory, every suggestion, was quickly and thoroughly discounted as if it had no merit whatsoever.

What is reasonable doubt? It has no real definition. It is relative and changes for each of us. The only definition we were given was some crap about it being "doubt that a reasonable person would have while engaging in the important affairs of life."

Whatever it meant, we were left to come up with some definition that would work for each of us—something we could live with. How sure did I have to be? Twenty percent? Fifty? Eighty? Ninety nine point nine percent? What was enough? How did I find the number I could live with?

What we "can live with" is completely different for each of us, but everyone else had gotten there. Why was it such a struggle for me? I had already admitted the guy was a bad husband and imperfect father who had killed Beth and hidden her body. So why couldn't I just find him guilty of first-degree intentional homicide? Why not? What was the big deal? Why couldn't I just set my percent of reasonable doubt really low, say around twenty percent, or even fifty percent, and let us all go home?

Because that's not why I was there. I had been given instructions and I was going to follow them. Why did I put myself through this three-week hell if I wasn't going to take it all the way? I just couldn't do it. I remembered thinking that if someone I loved were on trial, I'd want the jury to give him or her the full benefit of the law. If I had to find intent, I was not voting guilty until I was convinced. So I endured the struggle and tried to think. I replayed what we had agreed on:

- Dan had forced himself into the Jeep and coerced Beth to the 180.

- Dan and Beth had sex.
- Dan became enraged.
- Beth ended up dead.

I then began looking at possible scenarios:

- *Dan had killed Beth elsewhere, off the 180-acre property.* This was a scenario that we had discussed and discounted as possible, but unlikely. This scenario strongly suggested intent, because it meant that Dan had driven Beth somewhere else, undoubtedly against her will.
- *Dan had killed Beth at the 180-acre property via an intentional act.* Possibilities were numerous, but the most likely ones included smothering or strangulation. This scenario also implied intent.
- *Dan had killed Beth at the 180-acre property via some freak accident.* This one bothered me. In my head, a very easonable scenario was that Beth was walking or running away from Dan when he grabbed, tackled, or pushed her, and accidentally caused her death. It seemed unlikely, but that kind of thing does happen. A substantial part of me didn't really think that Dan wanted Beth dead. The more I believed that he didn't want her dead, the more plausible this scenario became.

Rick laid into me: "How can you be so set on one scenario and refuse to see ours?" I couldn't believe it. His anger hurt and was one of the most deflating experiences of my life. I felt like I was going to lose it, and then remembered he was a 20-year-old kid who should not have been here in the first place, and forced myself to calm down. I looked him in the eye and said, "Rick, trust me when I say that I see your points. All of them. I have listened intently to every word you have said. Just because I don't agree with you or happen to see other possibilities doesn't mean that I'm not listening to you. Do you understand?"

He understood, and I was immensely thankful.

During a short break, Carrie, Mary Jo, and Linda were compassionate and understanding. They came over and sat next to me. Quietly, without any anger, frustration, or impatience, they started telling me why and how they had reached the conclusion that Dan was guilty. They put their arms around my shoulders and said they understood. They demonstrated what we all promised we would do from the very beginning: treat each other with respect and give each other time.

When we returned from break, I tried to lighten things up with some humor. "We might be a hung jury," I said, "but at least we are a well-hung jury." It didn't get as much laughter as it deserved. A hung jury and mistrial were becoming more and more of a real possibility. Everyone despised the thought, including me. We were pretty sure of the answer, but decided we needed to ask the judge another question just to make sure.

> *"If the jury is able to reach a unanimous decision on three of the offenses, but unable to reach a unanimous decision on one, is it a mistrial or hung jury as to all of the offenses, or just to the one lacking unanimity?"*

The judge gave us one of his typically cryptic responses, but it led us to the answer. It said, "*Reread jury instruction 484.*" We reread the instruction, which very clearly stated that separate verdicts were required for each count when a defendant is charged with multiple counts. We read that to imply that we could find Dan guilty of three offenses even if we were unable to reach unanimity on the fourth.

That was good to know. I had been very concerned that if we were not able to reach consensus, the whole case would be a mistrial and everything would have to begin again. I did not want that to happen.

I needed time. I started developing hypotheses I thought would make sense and be reasonable. I applied weights to each of the hypotheses. We decided the four most likely ways for Dan to have killed Beth were:

- Strangulation
- Smothering
- Punch (either hard enough to kill her, which I doubted, or knocking her over where her head hit a solid part of the car or pavement)

- Push/Shove (again, where her head hit a solid part of the car or pavement)

I asked everyone for any other possible ways he could have killed her, and we came up with quite a list of possibilities, including poisoning, drowning, stabbing, running her over, etc. It was so appalling; we all wondered how we could talk about such things. Separation from reality.

Even though many other suggestions were made, most were ridiculous and I got increasingly frustrated and angry with people for wasting time. Of course, that is what they thought I was doing and "He could have just thrown her out of an airplane or run her over a few times with the Jeep" was just their way of telling me so.

The frustration and anger continued. I ignored those feelings as well as I could and kept working. I focused on strangulation, smothering, a shove, or a punch as the most likely possibilities. The first two I marked with an "I," meaning that intent would be easy enough to justify. The second two I marked with an "E," meaning there could either be intent or not. I did believe, though, that if Dan had killed Beth with a punch or a push, it was without intent and would have, in fact, been an accident.

It still seemed to me that the most likely was the shove. I was unable to see him punching Beth after twelve years of never physically abusing her.

Strangulation or suffocation could have occurred in a moment of rage; after all, we'd already decided that Dan was an incredibly desperate man. These options seemed wholly plausible and were what had led eleven jurors to vote guilty. For me, they were not enough.

I couldn't get the possibility of the shove and accidental death out of my head. It seemed plausible enough. What was the chance that an accident could have been her cause of death?

Several jurors looked at it this way: Beth was dead, so one could not look at Dan's act alone in deciding how likely it was. One also had to look at the result. Because Beth was dead, one had to assume that Dan had engaged in an activity that was more likely to kill her. This was a very interesting point and a good one. It strongly suggested that of our four main possibilities, suffocation or strangulation were the most likely.

However, the innocent-until-proven-guilty part of me, the part that sees reasonable doubt as an extremely high standard, couldn't look at it that way. This is not to say that I didn't understand and see their point—I did. To me, it was a backward way of analyzing this hypothesis. My take on it was this: Dan got enraged and did something.

It seemed just as plausible to me that something *without* intent to kill (whether it be a push or shove that caused her to fall and hit her head and die) was just as likely as something *with* intent (such as strangulation or suffocation).

I couldn't help but think that this could have happened. And if it did, I would guess that ninety-nine times out of one hundred, Beth would still be alive. I was looking at the cause, not the effect; the action, not the reaction. In my mind, this hypothesis seemed more likely. On the other hand, one could not ignore the fact that Beth was dead and the other jurors were using that information to take a reverse angle and reach a far different inference.

I was confused by the "accidental death in a rage hypothesis," and my fellow jurors were not lessening the pressure. I asked what they thought about the likelihood, or even possibility, that Dan had gone temporarily insane. No one had a response, so I proposed that we ask the judge:

> *"If the defendant is in such a rage as to be unaware of his actions and thus be unaware that his conduct is practically certain to cause death, even if a "reasonable" or "sane" person would have realized it in the same position, can we still find the defendant guilty of intent, or does this remove the possibility?"*

I continued to be berated while we waited. As usual, we were pretty sure that we knew the answer, but I, of course, still needed to hear it from the judge. Finally, a knock came at the door indicating that we had received a response.

> *"You are to follow only the instructions provided to you. There is no instruction regarding the defendant's mental status other than as set forth in the instructions that you have."*

This wasn't particularly clarifying. We thought we knew what it meant, and it validated what we had believed: there is no such thing as temporary insanity in this case. We remained locked in an all-or-nothing decision.

Once again, I started applying percentages to each action in which we presumed it was most likely for Dan to have engaged. My co-jurors could not fathom why I was wasting so much time; every new strategy I developed irritated them even more. Nonetheless, I took these percentages and applied them to the likelihood that that particular action would cause Beth to die. Without the second part, I probably never would have gotten beyond reasonable doubt. When I included the second part, and basically did what the other jurors had suggested, my scenarios became less and less likely.

But it still wasn't easy. I kept reminding people that accidents happen to people all the time. When you look at an individual, yes, it's unlikely that a freak fall will result in death. But when you look from a macro level, it's much more common. We were told that we could draw upon our experiences in life. I told the jurors about my godfather, who had been playing racquetball when he fell and hit his head. He'd probably done this a thousand times and never thought twice about it. But this time, he fell wrong. There was no blood, but he was in a coma for months. The fluke that no one believed ever happened, had happened recently to someone I knew and loved. Linda agreed, telling a story of her cousin who hurt himself playing ice hockey. There was no blood and he walked off the ice. He went home, went to sleep, and never woke up. Many of the jurors raised their eyebrows and shook their heads back and forth, as if I'd made the story up to try to sway their opinions.

Obviously, these real-life experiences were not enough to pull them back from beyond reasonable doubt. I wasn't even sure that was what I wanted. Was I trying to mitigate my uncertainty, to compromise? We had already ensured that this man was going to spend a long time behind bars. I still believed in the inherent goodness of people, and three weeks of misery couldn't change that. Was

I harboring doubt just because of my own fears and inability to orphan two children and send this man to prison for life?

There was no cause of death. We couldn't prove *anything*. I did not have any idea what to do. I couldn't objectively assess facts because there weren't any, and I didn't know how my own conscience was affecting my judgment. Was I just being indecisive out of fear? The constant pressure and frustration of the others was not making it any easier.

I asked what reasonable doubt meant to each of them, how sure they felt they had to be. Someone said seventy percent. Someone said eighty-five percent. Most of my fellow jurors said between ninety and ninety-five percent. One person said 99.9 percent. That was my number, too.

The other person had voted guilty. I hadn't arrived at that point yet.

There is no doubt in my mind that a defense mechanism rose up, allowing each juror to believe that he or she was right. It was just a natural response for each person to build a wall around their decision that ensured he or she was comfortable with it. How else could one live with oneself? I know how hard it is to live with that discomfort, and it seemed wholly reasonable that each juror would wrap himself or herself in the protective cloak of certainty regarding what was likely the most serious decision any of them had ever made.

But that doesn't change what happened. It doesn't change that I was a lone voice, trying to reach my own comfort level, respecting theirs, and having very little interest in being subjected to intense pressure to vote their way and let them go home. Mary never said a word. Carrie, Linda, and Mary Jo showed a great deal of respect. Everyone else wanted out.

The yelling, flaring tempers, and demonstrable frustration continued. My weights and percentages were bringing their anger to fever pitch.

One juror tried the patronizing approach. "Brian, dear, let me explain to you why we're so right…"

One juror called me a "zero." I think she was joking. I *hope* she was joking.

One juror tried to convince me that in order to be found not guilty, Dan had had to be thinking, while killing Beth, that his conduct was not likely to kill her. I disagreed completely, saying that Dan didn't have to be thinking anything. The juror had things backwards. If Dan was thinking that his conduct was not likely to kill her, or *even if Dan was thinking nothing*, we *had* to find him "not guilty."

The only way we could find Dan guilty of first-degree intentional homicide was to believe that he had mental purpose to kill or was aware that his conduct was practically certain to result in death. To me, it was the exact opposite of what the juror suggested and played more into the hands of a not guilty verdict than a guilty one. This line of thinking changed no one's mind, but at least it silenced the juror.

One of the jurors suggested that I vote guilty because the punishment for second-degree murder was close enough to the punishment for first-degree (sixty years for a 32-year-old amounted to life). I was incredulous. I was about to throw him across the room when he dropped the idea.

Finally, a couple jurors decided they'd had it, and all hell broke loose. Rules and respect disappeared. It was an all-out onslaught. Five jurors began screaming at once, people banged their fists on the table, and shook their heads in disgust. Things progressed from hurtful to horrible and it seemed that there would be no light at the end of the tunnel.

I couldn't think and didn't know how I would reach a decision. This went on for fifteen minutes. I could do nothing but stare in disbelief, until suddenly, the Rick I knew returned.

He'd been uncommonly quiet since we had talked about my perspective and why this was hard on me. I wanted so much for him to be on my side. He silenced the screaming and bickering by saying, "Brian said at the beginning, and I agreed, that we all needed to be absolutely comfortable with our decision when we left this room. I think we should all be quiet and give Brian time to think and reach whatever decision he needs to."

Order was restored instantly and everyone quietly agreed. I was unbelievably impressed with Rick's maturity. I was also very appreciative of Rick's idea, because that was exactly what I needed.

It was like a new world. Almost at once, there was complete silence, and I could feel myself breathe again. It was like I'd been released from a torture chamber. The silence lasted for a couple minutes, and then people just started quietly talking with each other. I read and reread the statutes and the jury instructions to myself. What did "intent" really mean? What exactly was "reasonable doubt"?

It was hard to concentrate. I knew eleven people wanted to go home. I knew there were only two possible results at this point: both rested squarely and completely upon my shoulders.

Guilty.

Hung jury and mistrial.

I was having a hard time concentrating because I knew the entire decision rested on my shoulders. All I could think about was what would happen if I needed another week to decide? I envisioned hours and days of frustration and anger, welling up more and more in my fellow jurors. All I could think about was how rankled they were. "If this goes on much longer," I said, "we're not going to have a hung jury; we're going to have a hung juror." Luckily, people laughed instead of searching for a rope.

Still, I felt their eyes boring into me and I couldn't concentrate on anything else. I finally picked up a chair and carried it, with the jury instructions and the statute, into the women's restroom and closed the door. I was in there about an hour or so, considering the meanings of each of these terms: intent and reasonable doubt, *mental purpose* and *conduct practically certain to cause death*.

Finally, I came out of the bathroom and walked back to the table. No one said a thing to me, thankfully, because I still wasn't ready. I replayed hypotheses, theories, possibilities. I applied percentages and reapplied them. I read the words written before me. I read them again. Finally, I started concentrating on the word *conduct*. There was something that, after all this time, led me to that word: an awareness that one is engaging in *conduct* that is practically certain to cause death.

I'd been taking the word *conduct* and applying it solely to those five seconds to five minutes between the time when Dan became enraged and Beth became dead. I decided to spread it out and apply it to Dan's conduct for the entire day.

I started with Dan's stalking. His switching cars. His secretive entry into Beth's Jeep. His forcing Beth to drive to the 180-acre property against her will. His coercing her to have sex with him against her will. Knowing this was probably the end of their marriage and the end of the land and becoming enraged when Beth confirmed one or both of those facts. Killing her. Hiding her body—a cowardly, heinous act that has left her family in even more pain than they should otherwise be. Lying to at least four police officers that night. Lying to his brother. Telling his brother, "You can have sex with them and they still leave you." And showing absolutely no emotion, regret, remorse, sadness, or concern through hours upon hours of interviewing and questioning, for either his wife of twelve years or his two children.

I believed all of the above. Before Beth died, Dan's conduct spoke to lies and misdirection. But I also had to look at Dan's conduct *after* Beth died. His lack of concern for his family leaned more toward intent than accident. I applied *conduct* to the entire timeline and decided that, when taken together, with everything else (the hypotheses, scenarios, testimony, and evidence), I could believe, beyond a reasonable doubt, that Dan should have been aware that his conduct was practically certain to result in Beth's death.

I thought about what to do. I was pretty sure I believed Dan should have been aware of his conduct. But sending someone to prison for life, essentially orphaning two children, was some heavy stuff. I remembered wondering, three weeks earlier, if I could send a man to prison for life. Here I was.

I thought about Dan Kutz, the man I now knew so well, rotting his life away behind bars. It made me sick. I thought about that potential juror, way back at the beginning, who said he could not judge other people. I remember thinking, "Dude, trust me, none of us relishes the idea." Well, here I was and it was time. And nothing else and no one else mattered. There was one judge and one jury and I was both. I looked around the room at my fellow jurors, all of whom were lost in their own worlds or talking to each other.

Very quietly, I said, "I can live with it."

A hush fell over the room and everyone looked at me. We had been deliberating for over twenty hours in the course of two days. The count had been eleven to one for just over four hours. I said, "I really didn't want to leave this room until I was comfortable, but I'm not ever going to be comfortable, with any decision. When I apply the word 'conduct' to his actions for the entire evening, I can get to intent, and I can live with it."

It was unanimous: twelve to zero.

Dan Kutz was guilty of first-degree intentional homicide.

Thirty-two

I felt sick, sicker than I had ever felt in my life. Somehow, the complete and utter silence in the room made it worse. My heart beat like the wings of a thousand geese taking flight simultaneously. My mind raced; had I done the right thing? Should I have taken a little longer? Was I completely certain? I was angry at everyone, angry at what had happened, wondering what the hell I'd been thinking when I had actually wanted to be on this jury.

Everyone else seemed to be wearing looks of resignation, disbelief, or concern. We had just sentenced a man to life in prison, and it looked to me like it had just hit some of them for the first time. I felt dreadful, but also felt some peace in the extent of my analysis. I wasn't sure if others felt that way or not.

We went around the room, one at a time, to share our final thoughts. Each juror said pretty much the same thing, in his or her own way. No one had come here with preconceptions or strong opinions one way or the other. Every one of us, through this process of deliberation, had reached, beyond reasonable doubt, a place where we could find this man guilty.

Dan Kutz had gotten an intelligent, well-reasoned, and conscientious jury. It may sound corny, but I believe it. The last four minutes, in that circle of final thoughts, had been a different universe than the last four hours. Once the frustration subsided, it was clear that no one had taken this decision lightly.

James read each of the counts, and we voted.

"Stalking?" Twelve hands went up. Guilty.

"Obstruction of justice?" Twelve hands went up. Guilty.

"Hiding a corpse?" Twelve hands went up. Guilty.

"First-degree intentional homicide?" Eleven hands went up. Feeling like I was going to pass out, with everyone looking at me, my hand slowly followed. Guilty.

James signed the guilty verdict forms as we voted.

We knocked on the door. Lori answered. We told her we were ready and had reached a decision.

The one thing we had craved most during this experience—home—was exactly what we had just stripped from this man.

Deliberations in the Dan Kutz murder trial were over.

We were going home, and he wasn't.

THIRTY-THREE

We lined up for the last time, and the door opened to "Please rise for the jury." It was the second-to-last time we would hear these words. Solemnly, the twelve of us entered the courtroom.

My head was bowed, but I couldn't help looking around to see who had managed to assemble in the brief forty-five minutes that had passed since we had knocked on the door and told the bailiff we were ready. I couldn't believe my eyes. The courtroom was completely packed. I thought about what people had been doing, what it would have been like on the outside for the last thirty-five hours. It was the first time, in all these hours, it had even crossed my mind. People waiting, praying. Beth's family—I couldn't begin to imagine what they must have been thinking all this time.

Questions raced through my head. What was going on with the media? Were there vans parked outside right now, waiting to get the first story? Reporters, photographers, writers, all doing what? Waiting? Watching? All this time in deliberations, I hadn't even thought about any of that. There had been no separation from reality. This time it was a complete break. I was shocked to realize that the thought of an outside world had not crossed my mind one single time during deliberations.

Kaiser, Opelt, and Searls were sitting at the prosecution table closest to us. Just past them, at the defense table, were Burke, Watson, and Dan Kutz. Behind the prosecution were all the faces we had come to recognize over the last eighteen days: Beth's mother and stepfather, father and stepmother, brothers, cousins, uncles, aunts, and close friends. They were all there, packed six or seven to a bench, filling the seven benches that extended from the prosecution's table back to the exit door.

The other side of the courtroom was full as well. Only a few people were recognizable as being "regulars," only a handful were known because they had testified: Dan's sisters, his brother John, other friends and family members. I felt waves of regret and uncertainty and sickness. I looked around and panicked. What had I just done?

I looked at Ellen Maier, Beth's mom, and wondered if she was going to raise Jacob and Jennifer now that I had orphaned them. I looked at Dan's sister, Kim, who'd come all the way down from northern Wisconsin to support her brother and testify for the defense. I liked her and I wanted to run over and beg her forgiveness.

I looked at Watson and Burke. I had no idea what was going through their minds. What did they think? Did they think we were on their side? Were they praying? I wanted to bring them back to the jury room and explain everything to them. I wanted them to know they'd done a good job.

I looked at Dan Kutz. I've read dozens of courtroom dramas, and it seems a pervasive myth that if the jury refuses to look at the defendant, it means they are going to find him guilty. I didn't know what to do. I didn't want to look at him, because I didn't want to get his spirits up in the remote chance that someone had told him that absolute untruth.

I couldn't help it. For what seemed like a lifetime, I had looked right in that man's eyes in an attempt to find some kind of sign. In all that time, I had failed. This time was no different— they betrayed nothing.

I wanted to apologize to him. I wanted to run up, shake him, and scream into his face, "Why?" I wanted to know where Beth was. My heart raced and my mind wordlessly voiced myriad questions to which I would never get answers. I couldn't take it anymore, so I closed my eyes and took a deep breath. Then I looked at the judge.

Stuart Schwartz was a good judge. We had all liked him immediately, way back on day one of jury selection. We had gotten to know him quite well and were all impressed with his intelligence, demeanor, and the way he ran his courtroom. I looked at him for the last time.

"Mr. Anderson, am I to assume that you are the foreman?"

James: "Yes, Your Honor."

Judge: "Mr. Foreman, has the jury reached a unanimous verdict on the four counts of the criminal information that have been charged?"

James: "We have, Your Honor."

Judge: "Bailiff, please bring me the verdict." The bailiff did so. The judge read the verdict. "On the count of first-degree intentional homicide, we, the jury, find the defendant, Daniel H. Kutz, guilty. Jurors, if you so find, please signify by raising your hand." Hushed cries from the audience. There was one distinct cry I recognized immediately, and will replay over and over in my head for the rest of my life. It was not happiness, nor anything nearing it, but for the first time since I'd met her almost three weeks earlier, I sensed something approaching relief from Ellen Maier.

For the second time in less than an hour, eleven hands went up and were slowly joined by another. "I can live with it," I reminded myself, "I can live with it."

"Mr. Burke," the judge asked, "would you like an individual poll of the jurors?"

"No, thank you, Your Honor," replied Burke.

Judge: "On the count of hiding a corpse, we, the jury, find the defendant, Daniel H. Kutz, guilty. Jurors, if you so find, please signify by raising your hand." Twelve hands immediately went up. More, louder cries from the audience. I looked around the courtroom again. Things were happening in slow motion. Dan still showed absolutely no emotion whatsoever. Beth's family was in tears, looking pleased, but far from peaceful. Justice was round one, but peace would not come until Beth was found.

"Mr. Burke," the judge asked, "would you like an individual poll of the jurors?"

"No, thank you, Your Honor," replied Burke. Burke was subdued, almost calm. He didn't look surprised.

Judge: "On the count of stalking, we, the jury, find the defendant, Daniel H. Kutz, guilty. Jurors, if you so find, please signify by raising your hand." Twelve hands up again. More cries and I looked at Dan's side of the courtroom. His sister was crying and my heart reached out to her. I was so confused. Inside that courtroom, all activity seemed to be in super-slow motion. Every sound in the courtroom was a single, clearly identifiable entity. Every look on every face was frozen as if time were incapable of ever moving forward again.

"Mr. Burke," the judge asked, "would you like an individual poll of the jurors?"

"No, thank you, Your Honor," the attorney replied once again.

Judge: "On the count of obstruction of justice, we, the jury, find the defendant, Daniel H. Kutz, guilty. Jurors, if you so find, please signify by raising your hand." For the fourth and final time, twelve hands were raised in unison.

"Mr. Burke," the judge asked, "would you like an individual poll of the jurors?"

"No, thank you, Your Honor," he replied.

"Ladies and gentlemen of the jury, I thank you for your service. You are now relieved of duty."

"Please rise for the jury." The last time. In a dream, while walking out, feeling as though I was in some terrible nightmare from which I could not awaken, I remember thinking, "I'm going to miss those words."

THIRTY-FOUR

Waves of confusion, frustration, anger, and sadness poured over me, making it hard for me to breathe. I walked into our jury room, deflated and defeated, sat on a couch, and buried my head in my hands. I raised my head long enough to see that no one else looked much better. We were all distraught; each lost in our own thoughts, doubts, and fears. I'm sure we all felt some relief though; finally, it was almost over.

I walked over to Mary Jo, Carrie, and Linda and thanked them for the patience and respect they had shown me. I hugged each of them. I asked Rick how he was doing, and he said he was okay. It was Thursday night, two days after his fourth semester of college had started without him.

Jurors milled around for awhile, checking on each other and talking about anything other than the case. Finally, Judge Schwartz came in to thank us, give us some general information, and answer any questions that we might have. I had a million, but little strength and nowhere near enough interest to ask any of them.

Someone asked why we had gotten such vague answers to our deliberation questions, and Schwartz had a good reason:

"Anything I answered, in the affirmative or the negative, or even slightly opinionated in any way, could give you the impression that I was trying to lead you to a certain conclusion." Unbelievable. I had never even thought about that, and it made perfect sense.

Someone else asked why we hadn't been offered the choice of second-degree murder. He said that was because it was "inconsistent with the defense. If you claim that you are innocent of killing someone at all, then it is certainly inconsistent with 'it was an accident'." The reason made some sense, but I didn't understand how first-degree murder would be any different. In fact, every charge ever filed would be inconsistent with a defense of, "I didn't do it." I hoped I'd one day get the opportunity to debate this point with the judge, over a beer.

A bailiff came in to tell us that an alternate juror was waiting outside and wanted to come in and listen to what the judge was saying. I hoped it would be Jessica, and it was. She sat on a couch, looking composed and curious. I walked over and sat next to her. It was good to see her and I wanted to tell her everything, including how lucky she was to have been chosen as an alternate.

We listened to the rest of what the judge had to say and then, as a group, tried to sneak out of there. Lori and Kurt helped us avoid detection by the media by leading us through some empty courtrooms and then through the service elevator. For the last time, we got in the van and rode quietly back to the hotel.

Lynne was waiting in the lobby. I don't think I've ever been so happy to see anyone in my life. I hugged her for about five minutes, the first time I had been able to do so in eighteen days without a bailiff watching over us. She'd had a hard time, too, living alone and taking care of everything for all those days. It was nice to be together again. It was nice to be done.

Saying goodbye to everyone was odd. We all hugged, and I realized that I liked all of my fellow jurors and a bond had formed with each of them. I walked to the parking lot and hugged Lori for a long time. I thanked her and really meant it.

Driving home with Lynne was a strange feeling. I had a powerful desire to drive, to be in control of something, even if it was only a car. I was so used to merely being a passenger. I had missed driving, missed having the freedom to control my own actions. Walking into my house, seeing my puppies again, was an incredible feeling.

I unpacked some stuff, apologized to Lynne (I knew she was going to be upset, but I had to do it), and drove to Jessica's house.

It was too much, being in that room for all those hours, wondering how different things would have been if she had been there. I had to know. One different name pulled out of a hat, and everything could have been different. I would never have been able to sleep that night if I hadn't found out. I spent an hour telling Jessica what had happened. I told her about stalking, obstruction, murder, and hiding a corpse. I told her what it was like. Finally, I told her why we'd come to the conclusions we had and how I had reached "intent."

I asked her if she could have gotten there. I had to know. Thankfully, she said yes. I went back home and tried to explain everything to Lynne. She said yes, too.

I needed to hear it from both of them that night. I needed validation, needed to hear from someone else that what I had done made sense. I didn't sleep well, plagued by nightmares of loss and pain, but I slept. It was nice to be home again, falling asleep and waking up with Lynne.

And I didn't even need a wake-up knock.

PART FOUR:

Life Goes On

(The Post-Trial Search for Truth)

THIRTY-FIVE

It is hard to describe the bond you develop with people when you've spent the three hardest, most stressful weeks of your life together. I had spoken to so many people who wanted to know everything: at work, at the store, on the telephone. They wanted to know it all, what it was like and how hard it was to be sequestered.

"Was it hard to find someone guilty of murder?" They all wanted to know. Well, actually, yes, it was.

I missed the other jurors. It was two days after the trial, the first Saturday of the rest of my life, and Lynne and I went to see the movie "Crouching Tiger, Hidden Dragon." I couldn't help comparing the poignant sadness of the movie to what I had just experienced: three weeks of ruined marriages, tragic love stories, orphaned children, murdered wives, and grieving families. A tale of such incomprehensible sadness that I could barely stand to hear it.

I was painfully reminded that perhaps the biggest tragedy of being sequestered is having your support structure removed. A lot of jurors became friends with each other—it's almost impossible not to when you spend every waking second together for eighteen straight days. However, despite the new relationships that undoubtedly formed on this journey, I wondered whether they were little more than a reaction, a survival mechanism that helped us make it through.

I didn't know whether I would stay friends with Jessica, Rick, Timmy, or any of the rest of them, but that didn't negate the importance of what we were for each other at the time.

The movie was amazing: the cinematography, the music, the acting, the artistry, everything. It was the resolute sadness with which I found myself most closely identifying. I now understood how a story about loss and wasted time could hit so hard, like a swift kick in the gut.

After the movie, I put my arm around Lynne, leaned my head on her shoulder, and cried for what seemed like hours. I wept more intensely than I had since I was nine years old, twenty-three years earlier. I knew only fifteen other people who might have been able to understand what that felt like. I had only spoken to Jessica and that didn't even count because she hadn't been there at the end.

I thought about the eleven jurors with whom I had taken this all the way and hoped that they were okay. Were they happy and confident and comfortable? Or were they having the same nightmares that I was, even while awake? I hoped they were not. I hoped they were out there explaining their experience as heroes, with incredible stories of stoic bravery, thoughtful reasoning, and disturbing but deliberative justice. I hoped that they felt that way, because they deserved it. I deserved it. We were brave. We were thoughtful. We were reasonable and deliberate. We took no decision lightly.

During the trial, I had cried every day. These few days following the trial, it wasn't taking much to make the same thing happen. The day before, Friday, it had been a woman at work asking if it was hard to convict a man of murder. On Saturday, it was just a movie.

Maybe on Sunday, it would just be a thought or a dream.

Maybe this would be the last day. Maybe.

On Sunday, three days after the trial ended, I was walking around handing out our neighborhood quarterly newsletter. I saw neighbors, people I knew but not well enough for them to know where I had been for the past three weeks, or even that I was missing at all. They asked how I was doing, and I tried to lie but was unable to do a very convincing job. My typical answer was, "Still recovering," which, of course, led to the inevitable question, "From what?"

Jessica had told me while we were talking one night during the trial, "Girls know the best way to make themselves feel better. They just keep talking about something, and eventually they feel better." Jessica and I started calling it, "Doing the girl thing." During the trial, we had to invoke the "girl thing" on a pretty regular basis. Talking *did* help. It was hard to explain what it was like being a juror, being the center of attention wherever we went. In actuality, we were nothing more than prisoners, but we were treated like royalty. We were special, different. I was not sure that I would want this for the rest of my life, but for a couple weeks, it had been exciting.

In the courthouse, people parted wide to let us pass. In the restaurants, others stared as we marched solemnly by. At the elevator, they stood and waited for the next one because they couldn't ride with us. We were constantly shadowed by two armed bodyguards whose sole purpose was to protect us from being touched, talked to, or engaged in any other manner.

And so, when my neighbors asked me from what I was recovering, there was a part of me still searching for something when I answered, "I was a juror on the Dan Kutz murder trial." Of course, I never got what I needed. They'd say, "Wow" or "Whoa, I'd like to hear about that experience some time." To them, I was just the same old Brian. But I really wasn't—he was gone.

I was already a completely different person. I knew early on that I would never get over this experience, but as I looked at my neighbors and yearned for one more minute of stardom, I hoped that one day my life could fade, like everyone else's, into the quiet calm of anonymity, into a semblance of normalcy. Walking away with the disappointment that they had been unable to fulfill my ridiculous needs, I knew that that day was yet to come.

The weight of the decision had rested squarely on my shoulders and, four days after the trial ended, that feeling had yet to subside. There was no good reason for this—it had been twelve people in that room making a decision, not just one. No matter how many angles from which I chose to view the truth, I couldn't convince myself.

From the time Mary Jo had changed her vote and I was alone, to the end of deliberations, to reading the verdict, and up to this very minute, I knew, and know, that only two possibilities could emerge with regard to the charge of first-degree murder: finding Dan Kutz guilty of murder or causing a hung jury and a mistrial.

Those were the only two choices. I tried to tell myself otherwise, but I couldn't help but feel that I alone had sentenced this man to life in prison and orphaned his two young children. I knew it was crazy, but that didn't change the feeling deep in the pit of my stomach that refused, even after four days, to dissipate.

I couldn't help but wonder if my co-jurors had been as confident or if some natural defense mechanism had settled in. Many of them had acted so brazenly, supremely *positive* that they were right. Had I become their enemy because they needed validation? Because, given the severity of the decision, any doubts, even legitimate ones raised by another juror, were just too much to take? There was simply no way to know the truth. Because we couldn't be absolutely positive, we had to convince ourselves that we were.

Sitting here on my fourth day of freedom, I wondered if my eleven counterparts were still convinced. Because I wasn't. I had reached this conclusion of my own free will and could live with it. I looked at Kutz's conduct for that night, and it screamed intent. I looked at scenarios, possibilities, and probabilities. They screamed intent. I ran through explanation after hypothesis after theory.

Intent, intent, intent.

However, just because I could live with the decision, just because I was able to reach some relative standard known as reasonable doubt, didn't mean I was completely comfortable with it, and that lack of comfort has remained to this day. I remembered announcing to my fellow jurors that I could live with a guilty verdict, and I remembered the looks in their eyes. It was like some part of them wanted to back up, to vote again, to ask themselves what they were thinking and whether they were absolutely sure about what they were doing.

I'm not sure what look I was wearing, but I *was* confident that I had done my own analysis. I had reviewed the instructions and the definitions and the statutes until they were ingrained in my mind, had played with meanings and changed word structures and, ultimately, had gotten there.

Somewhere in the midst of deliberations, I came to the realization that I was never going to leave that room comfortable, no matter what we decided. It had now been four days, and I still wasn't comfortable. I hoped that maybe one day I would be.

I received an e-mail at work five days after the trial ended. It was from a co-worker who wanted to thank me for "sitting on that jury and being away from your family for [such a] long time period." She had grown up next to Beth and her parents and had taught Beth in Sunday School.

This was something I hadn't expected. It had never crossed my mind that anyone I knew would know Dan, Beth, or anyone associated with this case. I nervously read on, "Beth's family is quiet, good people who have a strong, stable background and mind their own business. No matter how you voted or reacted, I felt better knowing that a juror with your personality and brains was there doing the right thing."

It was the most thoughtful thing anyone had said to me since this whole thing began. I couldn't articulate how much it meant to have someone thank me for what I had done, to tell me that no matter what decision I'd reached, they were sure I'd done the right thing. Of course Lynne and Jessica had said that, and later, I'd have other good friends who would say the same thing. But this was different—this was someone detached from the whole thing, detached from me, going out of their way to thank me for what I had done. It was an amazing feeling, and I found myself reading and rereading the e-mail. In some indescribable way, it was the first day I was able to start reconnecting with the world.

My co-worker concluded: "My parents asked me to tell you thank you for giving up a month of your life for this. We all cried when we heard the verdict."

My e-mail response to her was, "It was the hardest thing I've ever done in my life, and you know how I voted, because we had to be unanimous. Thanks so much for your e-mail; it really helps. I am still struggling with this thing: not just the case and the sequestering, but also deciding what to do. It's a terrible thing; I wouldn't wish it on anyone. If you do know Beth's family, though, or ever have occasion to run into them, please tell them that there isn't a juror in the bunch who will not live with some of their pain every day for the rest of our lives. I've never met Beth, but I feel like I know her as well as a sister. I cried when I heard the verdict, too, and I already knew what it was."

Six days after the verdict, I was answering yet another round of questions about the trial, and soon, ten people were gathered around listening to my answers on the justice system and the good, bad, and ugly of reasonable doubt, murder charges, circumstantial evidence, the process of deliberations, and just about everything else about the case. No one on earth knew more about this case than select members of the family, the attorneys, Dan Kutz, the judge, and the fifteen other jurors who were probably facing this same conundrum every day. It was a strange feeling, and because the knowledge was so close and so intense, it was hard to remember that it was not commonplace. At the same time, I was struggling with the fact that, in spite of how much I knew, I didn't really know a damn thing. No one knew except Dan. He was the only one.

I hoped after the appeal was filed and denied that he would come forward and tell this family where he put Beth. I thought back to the testimony and tears, and imagined the uncertainty, fear, and questions that had become central to their lives. I thought back to the maps, the ten-minute horror they had represented for me, and the ongoing horror they represented for Beth's family. I could scarcely bear to imagine it. There was so much pain with no end in sight. They deserved peace. They deserved to know. It was six days later, and this thought consumed me more than any other. Every time another person asked me about the trial, it was feelings about Beth's family that continued to blur my vision.

A week after the trial ended, it still felt like only hours had passed. In other ways, though, it already seemed like a lifetime. I thought back to that life and remembered what it was like to spend every minute with the same people, hear about terrible things all day long, and have all semblance of free will taken from me. I remembered what it was like to be without Lynne, my dogs, and my freedom.

I remembered, but it was finally starting to seem like someone else's life, like a story I had heard and somehow memorized and could recount as if it were my own.

Things were finally starting to get better. I had yet to sleep straight through the night, but my nightmares were getting less frequent and less severe. That made my days better, too. I hadn't cried in three days.

I still wondered about my decision. I still stressed over it. I still wanted to call Beth's family and tell them how sorry I was. I still wanted to shake Dan until he admitted he had done it. Or hadn't. Or something. I wanted to know the truth.

When I started writing this book, the day following the conclusion of the trial, I wrote about the search for truth and how it was an individual thing. In the deliberation room, that was true. Out here, in the real world, there only remained one truth and the need to verify that the one we found was right.

A week had helped the trial fade slightly and allowed me to get through a day without tears, but the truth we had reached and the role we had played in its inevitable effect would be with me forever. I knew that as long as I lived, I would never get over this trial or forget what I had done. But I also knew, for my sake and everyone else's involved, finding the one remaining truth would certainly help.

Finding Beth. That was all that was left.

Thirty-six

Here is the test to find whether your mission on Earth is finished: if you're alive, it isn't.
Richard Bach

Fall seven times, stand up eight.
Japanese proverb

Two weeks after the end of the trial, Jessica and I went to a local pub to play some pool and have a few drinks. We never made it to pool; we had so much to talk about. It was an odd feeling. We'd talked on the phone since the trial ended, but this was the first time we'd seen each other in thirteen days, ever since I had gone to her house just following the verdict to get reassurance that I had done the right thing.

It was odd seeing each other in public, without guards or jurors or rules. We toasted our third drink as if it were something magical; we'd of course been unable to get more than two each for the entirety of the time we'd known each other. It was surreal being in this place. The last two times we had been here, in this very pub, we had been flanked by bodyguards and adorned with little red juror tags. We had been led immediately to the basement and kept isolated from the rest of the restaurant. The last time we had been here, we were in prison.

This time, we were free.

Of course, we talked about the trial and how we were both doing. Two weeks was not enough to remove it from my mind, and I was still thinking about it all the time and still waking up at night. But it happened less and less. It had gotten easier to say, "It's really hard to send someone to prison for the rest of his life and orphan two children." I would still choke up when I said it, but my mouth quivered less and less and I could get through the statement without feeling like I was going to lose it any second.

I knew I was doing better. Time had carried my memories and my hurt to a place where it was much more difficult to find them, to a place where I was not healed, but healing. It had been two weeks, and I was there. Jessica was doing well, too. We were there as friends and because we wanted to be, not because we had been forced to. We talked about work, significant others, vacations, and music and were able to just "be."

However, there was one feeling that had not diminished for either one of us. We wanted Beth to be found and for Beth's family to find peace.

I thought back to the pain and suffering and profound sadness with which we had been embraced on a constant basis. I shook my head in disbelief just thinking about it. But like creatures everywhere through the history of time, it takes a lot to keep down the spirit.

Spirit is a powerful thing, and it endures. Subjugated, conquered, and mastered, humans have always endured. I knew that in time, I would endure. I hoped that Beth's family would as well.

EPILOGUE

The pure and simple truth is rarely pure
and never simple.
Oscar Wilde

There are many flaws in our justice system. In a world that is far from perfect, we should recognize, acknowledge, and live with man's inability to create a perfect system. Forcing people to go through what we endured, while simultaneously and thoroughly separating them from their support system, is asking too much. To ask them to make life and death decisions is a heavy burden to bear, and I have to wonder whether it would be possible to develop a better way. Perhaps more phone calls or visits. Perhaps a little more freedom. Perhaps a little trust that jurors are not interested in being tampered with; that jurors want, as much or even *more* than anyone else, to get it right.

It is completely and entirely beyond the capacity of the judicial system to cope with a deliberation in which the jurors are eleven against one. The whole process is focused, in its entirety, on unanimity at whatever cost.

I can't begin to imagine how many men have been sent to prison because someone caved. Because the pressure was too intense and the other jurors wanted to go home. Because, locked away in a room with eleven strangers who are positive that they are right and are beyond ready to be finished, it is hard to stand up for yourself and what you believe.

There is something inherently flawed in a system that prides itself on its reliability, when there are numerous cases where it does not and cannot exist. I don't know the answer; I don't know if there *is* an answer.

There have been calls for transcribed deliberations, and several television stations have videotaped and broadcast jury deliberations in the past. I believe that the process, and the importance of jury secrecy, protection, and anonymity, are too important to broadcast.

At the same time, the process is imperfect, and by granting unimpeachable power to the jury, there is a built-in acceptance of that imperfection. Why? Why not develop a solution that could perhaps serve to provide the accountability that we demand from the rest of the judicial system, and *all* of our government systems, while simultaneously protecting the importance of secrecy and anonymity?

Perhaps transcriptions, video tapes, or other recordings, which would only be suitable for limited review, would help in some cases. However, I am not convinced that in the case of eleven to one, they would provide any assistance. Why would one juror who was too shy to stand by his or her case in private be less inclined to do so with a tape recorder in the room? It does not seem likely to me that the person would, and thus, the result would be exactly the same.

Another possibility would be that, upon the jury reaching eleven to one, some other process is triggered. A facilitator might help. Perhaps breaking the jury into small groups (and letting the sole hold-out address three jurors at a time in a different room) would help.

Perhaps not. This goes back to the same issue, that a juror would still need the fortitude and strength to stand before his or her other jurors, facing eleven sets of tired, frustrated eyes, and say, "No, I am not ready."

I do believe these suggestions could be helpful and should at least be considered as options. In the end, though, I think the only solution that would help in this case is for the judicial system to accept the magnitude of this flaw. Should that be recognized, there would be two possible solutions that I could see:

The first would be to change the unanimous requirement. Perhaps a two-thirds majority could be required, or even an eleven-to-one majority. Either way, it would allow a juror to stay true to his or her conscience without cracking beneath the burden of pressure from the other jurors. Unanimity is a standard that we seldom, if ever, call for in our other institutions, and there is little reason I can think of as to why this should be different. A simple majority is more than enough for the remainder of our important affairs in government and life. Why not here?

The second possible solution would be to develop an acceptance of mistrials. To face the reality that they can happen and that they are not necessarily the end of the world. The judge could inform jurors, from the beginning, that they absolutely have to do the best they can to reach unanimity. They must debate, argue, discuss, and review. The court will recognize, however, that it is sometimes impossible to arrive at a unanimous decision. The court recognizes that jurors are under extreme pressure to agree with each other. Because that is the standard set by our legal system (unless it were changed as suggested above), we must abide by that requirement. However, should the jurors be unable to reach unanimity, it merely states that the prosecution, or the defense, did not do a good enough job.

In a criminal trial, the prosecution must prove, beyond a reasonable doubt, that their position is legitimate. They must not merely do so for themselves or their clients. They must do so for the jury—the entire jury. If they cannot do so, they have not succeeded in doing their job and should go back to the drawing board and try again. This would be costly, time-consuming, and frustrating, but might improve this critical flaw.

In the end, we must find a way to balance jurors' privacy and anonymity needs, accountability of the system, the defendant's absolute right to fairness, and each juror's right to go home *accepting* the decision he or she had reached, regardless of whether the juror is comfortable with that decision or not.

Maybe we don't question this process because we are frightened of the truth. Maybe we are scared that admitting the severity of this flaw might call two centuries of verdicts into question.

Either way, the justice system needs to realize that forced unanimity is *not* unanimity—merely a mistrial in disguise. Everyone goes home, duties performed, and the system has prevailed yet again. But those twelve people know.

Let me be resoundingly clear: *This is not what happened in our case.* I reached my decision of my own free will and was willing to live with it. But I am outspoken and I discuss and debate major decisions every day. I have strong values and ideals and am willing to stick to them, no matter what anyone thinks or says. But I know so many people who don't have the strength. I know so many people who are just too shy or too concerned about what other people think. I know too many people who are just too afraid of confrontation.

If anyone like that had been in my shoes, he or she would have caved *instantly*. I don't mean to sound arrogant, but there is no doubt in my mind. And by caving, they would not have reached the level of analysis that I reached. They would not have taken four hours to review everything a hundred different ways until they'd come up with something they could live with. As sad and horrified as I was because of what I'd done, I couldn't begin to imagine what a person who had caved to the pressure would have felt.

That is a flaw in our system. A defendant deserves better than that. No matter how heinous his crimes, no matter how sure the rest of the world is of his guilt, he deserves better. Our system is founded and built upon this principle. It is also a flaw because a juror should never have to go home feeling worse than I did that night. And I can't imagine how many countless times that one has done exactly that.

What is truth, really? After all these weeks of soul searching and analysis, the only conclusion I can reach is that it doesn't exist. We think it does, and on some level, that's really important. But in reality, we shouldn't continue to fool ourselves.

Reasonable doubt. That makes more sense. I can't define it, but I can accept it. No one can truly define it, because it's different for everyone. If you think about it, it's perfectly reflective of the life we lead, the world in which we live. A standard of truth exists for everything, and it's different for each person. Truth is relative, changing, and impermanent. It therefore cannot be defined.

So many rock-solid truths have been shredded like confetti: the Earth is the center of the universe, the sun revolves around us, the Earth is flat, enslaving others is acceptable, and so many more that it's impossible to count or even imagine them all. Every truth is *the* truth, until someone proves it wrong. Everything is relative, based on time, culture, science, facts, opinions, evidence, money, and passion. Any one of these things could take truth and flip it on its head, rendering a completely different picture: a *new* truth.

There are places where truth can exist on some level. A mother's love for her children. The joy of a family on a picnic. Flying a kite. Three friends hacking in an old, beat-up jury room. Everywhere else, it is a fallacy. I'm not going to try to fool myself or anyone else into believing that we, the jurors, found truth. So when the judge said, "Don't search for doubt; search for the truth," he's kidding himself and everyone else.

A different jury, even one different juror out of twelve, could have spun any supposedly preordained truth like a top and come up with a completely different decision. It's hard to discuss, but it cannot be denied. This is not simply my trial, this is *any* trial. This is the single greatest flaw in our justice system, but one that cannot possibly be corrected.

Because unlike eleven to one, this is not a flaw in the system. This is a flaw in *life*.

One of many. Bad things happen to good people all the time, and this was no different. Beth Kutz deserved to die no more than a father with cancer or a starving child.

It is a flaw in life.

When we grieve for Beth, we grieve for this flaw. And we wonder, with all this supposed truth, why must we be surrounded with such pain?

Maybe it is to help us find truth in something. In the fact that life is short and can be ripped out from beneath us in a heartbeat and we need to cherish and treasure every second. Because it can all disappear so quickly and so unexpectedly. Just like the truth.

So in life and the search for truth, we perform the same function and are stricken with the same inevitable reality: *we do the best we can and hope we get it right.*

Really, we have little choice.

Beth Kutz is somewhere and her spirit is living and breathing with a new magic, a new soul, and a new heart. I can find her there. And there, in that place, I can find truth. And know I got it right.

ACKNOWLEDGEMENTS

Being a sequestered juror in a murder trial was a life-altering experience in many ways. I will never be the same person I was before the trial. But like all things, that is not necessarily bad. The trial, the experience, the bonds I made and the pain I felt, were all part of the journey that is life. Like all experiences—good, bad, or ugly—it is one I will always cherish; it brought me to where I am right now, and there's no place I'd rather be.

I have not kept in touch with any of the other jurors, except an occasional e-mail. Timmy is the only juror I talked to who gave me permission to use his name; everyone else's has been changed.

Writing a book has been an amazing journey and I am thankful to everyone who has helped support me.

Thank you, Lynne. You are my best friend and life mate. Thanks for delivering clean undies, visiting me, supporting me, and being here when I got back. It has been a hard road, but we've survived the potholes and made it. I have found, in my love for you, a truth that is not ever-changing, relative, or impermanent. It is as real as the sun and as easy to describe.

Thanks to all of my readers and editors who have given me hope and confidence along the way. Special thanks to Lacy Werner, Kira Henschel, Lynne Solomon, Rachel O'Konis, Robin Haley Fischer, Jane DeRosia, Deb Schwid, Jill French, Chelsey Heller, and all my other family and friends who have read my book, made suggestions, and kept me inspired.

To the Dane County Deputy Sheriffs (Lori, Tom, Kurt, Paula, and Aaron): thanks for doing your best to make prison bearable—in fact, almost fun. Try to find a couple of vegetarian restaurants next time.

To my fifteen co-jurors: in spite of it all, a diligent, intelligent, reasoned, and objective jury.

To Ms. Hackman and Hackman, Jr.: a hack, a set of juggling balls, two guitars, a broken bulletin board, a choad, an uncoordinated chicken, three kids gathered around a set of duct-taped headphones, a sparrow in spring, and numerous pissed-off jurors.

Dan Kutz has appealed the guilty verdicts, and as of this writing, our decision has been upheld. Beth has still not been found, and Dan has yet to say a word. I have spoken with Beth's family on numerous occasions. They know that my heart is with them and that this book has been written in large part with them in mind. I look forward to one day meeting them in person, sharing a beer, and talking about happier things.

Ellen, Beth's mother, is raising the kids, Jacob and Jennifer. She has told me that she is raising them the way she thinks Beth would have wanted her to.

As we get close to publication, it has been more than five years since Beth disappeared. I still think about her often. Beth's family continues to search for her. Until they find her, I think it likely they always will. They remain in my thoughts. I still have hope that they will find closure and move on with their lives.

I'm not sure where it comes from, perhaps from the pain we have shared over a common occurrence, perhaps from the strange but indelible feeling that Beth was a member of my family, but I still feel a certain amount of love for her family, and I guess that I always will.

About the Author

Brian Solomon lives with his wife, his daughter, and two dogs in Madison, Wisconsin. He is the author of numerous essays, articles, and works of poetry. This is his first book.

kaiya + Tamirat
2148 West Lawn Ave
Madison, WI 53711
608·294·9289